The Attributes of God

*A Solemn and Blessed Contemplation
of Some of the Wondrous and
Lovely Perfections of the
Divine Character*

By ARTHUR W. PINK

REINER PUBLICATIONS

Swengel, Pennsylvania

FOREWORD

"Acquaint now thyself with Him, and be at peace: thereby good shall come unto thee" (Job 22:21). "Thus saith the Lord, Let not the wise man glory in his wisdom, neither let the mighty glory in his might, let not the rich glory in his riches: But let him that glorieth glory in this, that he understandeth, and knoweth Me, that I am the Lord" (Jer. 9:23,24). A spiritual and saving knowledge of God is the greatest need of every human creature.

The foundation of all true knowledge of God must be a clear mental apprehension of His perfections as revealed in Holy Scripture. An unknown God can neither be trusted, served, nor worshipped. In this booklet an effort has been made to set forth some of the principal perfections of the Divine character. If the reader is to truly profit from his perusal of the pages that follow, he needs to definitely and earnestly beseech God to bless them to him, to apply His Truth to the conscience and heart, so that his life will be transformed thereby.

Something more than a theoretical knowledge of God is needed by us. God is only truly known in the soul as we yield ourselves to Him, submit to His authority, and regulate all the details of our lives by His holy precepts and commandments. "Then shall we know, if we follow on (in the path of obedience) to know the Lord" (Hosea 6:3). "If any man will do His will, he shall know" (John 7:17). "The people that do know their God shall be strong" (Dan. 11:32).

—ARTHUR W. PINK.

TABLE OF CONTENTS

Foreword ....

The Solitariness of God   1

The Decrees of God   7

The Knowledge of God 13

The Foreknowledge of God 19

The Supremacy of God 27

The Sovereignty of God 32

The Immutability of God 38

The Holiness of God 43

The Power of God 50

The Faithfulness of God 58

The Goodness of God 65

The Patience of God 70

The Grace of God 76

The Mercy of God 83

The Love of God 90

The Wrath of God 96

The Contemplation of God 103

AUTHORS CITED

Author	*Page Number*
Bishop, G. S.	82
Booth, Abraham	76
Brine, John	94
Charnock, Stephen	41, 43, 44, 44, 46, 48, 50, 52, 71, 71
Dick, John	42, 106, 108
Edwards, Jonathan	11
Gurnall, William	101
Haldane, Robert	98
Hervey, James	54, 79
Howe, John	44, 104
Manton, Thomas	65
Spurgeon, Charles	32, 52, 69, 104

SCRIPTURES CITED

Reference	Page	Reference	Page	Reference	Page
Genesis		Exodus		I Kings	
1:	53	33:19	83	3:6	83
1	1	"	104	17:	30
31	45	34:6	70		
"	66	7	87	II Kings	
2:16	35	24	30	6:5	30
6:3	73	Leviticus			
6	39	10:3	48	I Chronicles	
8	81			29:11,12	29
8:22	17	Numbers			
"	59	14:	30	II Chronicles	
15:13-16	59	17	72	20:6	29
16:13	18	18	70	21	43
22:16	99	23:19	39	33:	79
49:4	40	"	59		
		32:23	14	Nehemiah	
Exodus				9:5	2
3:5	48	Deuteronomy		17	72
14	38	1:34	99		
22	36	7:7,8	91	Job	
12:35	36	9	58	5:19	64
41	59	9:24	22	8:11	54
14:	29	29:18-20	88	9:8	53
15:11	1	32:4	38	11:7-9	103
"	43	39-41	97	22:2,3	106
"	57	43	100	14	53
19,20,24	35	Joshua		21	iii
33:17	22	10:	30	23:10	14
19	77	I Samuel		13	29
"	81	15:19	39	"	40
				26:14	4

Reference	Page	Reference	Page	Reference	Page
Job		Psalms		Psalms	
26:14	52	50:21	100	119:75	63
"	104	52:1	65	89	39
35:7,8	3	57:10	88	138	61
38:4-6	52	59:16	83	130:3	100
11	55	62:11	50	135:6	30
42:3	29	66:9	40	"	33
		"	54	136:1	83
Psalms		78:65	39	"	85
1:5	101	86:5	83	15	87
2:4	29	15	70	25	66
2:9	28	89:6	51	139:2-4,6	13
7	7	7	48	14	66
"	24	8	58	23,24	15
11	48	11-13	53	143:12	87
12	56	32-33	63	145:8	71
"	88	35	44	9	67
4:6,7	107	"	99	"	76
5:5	47	90:8	14	"	84
7:11	47	93:3,4	56	15,16	66
"	97	95:11	99	17	45
"	102	97:12	100	146:3	41
9:17	87	98:1	44	147:5	15
16:2,3	3	99:5	48	150:1	54
18:13-15	51	100:5	39	Proverbs	
19:8,9	45	103:1	44	3:32	46
22:3	46	8	72	15:3	18
27:1	57	11	88	26	46
4	44	14	15	16:9	31
30:4	44	17	83	19:21	16
31:15	31	104:3	53	21:1	30
33:5	66	24	9	21:30	29
33:9	53	105:42	44	Ecclesiastes	
11	40	107:8	69	3:14	37
36:5	59	110:3	44	7:29	45
6	54	115:3	29	8:11	72
37:7	31	"	33	Song of Solomon	
50:21	27	116:5	85	8:6,7	94
"	46	119:68	66		

Reference	Page	Reference	Page	Reference	Page
Isaiah		Daniel		Matthew	
2:22	41	4:34,35	108	5:48	75
6:3	44	35	16	7:23	22
7:14	60	"	32	8:3	51
11:5	59	"	51	15:14	79
27:11	85	7:10	84	20:15	32
30:18	61	9:7	63	"	68
38:8	30	11:32	iii		
40:13,14	10			Mark	
15-18	4	Hosea		14:33	101
22,23	4	5:15	63	61	3
45:9	34	6:3	iii	62	52
46:10	10	7:2	14		
"	32	8:4	22	Luke	
50:10	60			1:78	83
53:10-12	36	Amos		"	86
54:10	41	3:2	22	2:14	68
57:20	40			52	11
64:6	47	Nahum		12:5	102
65:24	15	1:2	46	32	37
		3	71	13:3	88
Jeremiah		7	69	17:10	3
1:5	22			24:44	17
7:13	39	Habakkuk			
9:23,24	iii	1:13	43	John	
12:5	101	3:4	52	1:17	80
31:3	39	17,18	107	18	99
"	92			3:3	5
		Zechariah		16	93
Lamentations		12:10	82	"	95
3:22,23	59			18	81
24	106	Malachi		34	95
		3:6	1	4:24	5
Ezekiel		"	38	"	90
8:18	42	"	104	7:17	iii
11:5	14			10:14	22
22:14	56	Matthew		13:1	39
28:15	45	3:7	101	"	94
		"	102	7	61
Daniel		5:45	85	21:17	15
2:22	13				

Reference	Page	Reference	Page	Reference	Page
Acts		Romans		Ephesians	
2:23	7	8:32-39	94	1:4	26
"	17	"	95	4,5	92
"	22	9:12	97	"	93
"	24	15	85	5	2
9:1	80	18	37	6	48
13:18	73	9:19	93	9	7
46	74	22	56	11	1
48	20	"	72	"	8
14:16,17	73	23	88	"	10
15:18	7	11:2	23	"	31
"	16	5	25	"	32
17:23	4	"	26	2:4	93
25	84	6	77	4,5	88
18:27	25	29	40	8,9	25
"	26	33	10	"	77
20:24	81	34,35	2	3:11	7
		36	12	19	94
Romans		"	31	20,21	57
1:18	98	15:5	72	5:2	73
19-26	73				
2:4	69	I Corinthians		Colossians	
2:5	68	1:9	62	1:10	6
3:	55	2:14	5	16	106
8	88	6:9-11	80	2:9	99
19	81	8:3	22	10	34
24	77	11:30	62	"	84
4:4,5	77	13:12	105	3:12	73
5:15,17,21	81	II Corinthians		I Thessalonians	
21	77	1:3	89	1:10	99
"	94	4:6	5	5:23	49
7:12	45	5:11	102	24	63
8:	98	13:4	11		
7	14	Galatians		II Thessalonians	
28	7	4:4	60	2:13	10
"	12	4,5	68	"	24
29	24				
29,30	23	Ephesians		I Timothy	
30	63	1:4	9	1:17	108

Reference	Page	Reference	Page	Reference	Page
I Timothy		Hebrews		II Peter	
5:21	34	6:17	40	2:5	73
"	84	9:22	46	3:9	74
6:16	4	10:14	37	18	5
		23	60		
II Timothy		12:6	95	I John	
1:9	9	28,29	99	1:5	43
"	77	29	61	"	65
"	91			"	90
12	64	James		"	95
13	24	1:17	16	4:8	90
19	37	"	38	"	95
2:13	58	"	94	19	91
19	22	2:13	67	5:14	41
"	63	4:13,15	31		
		I Peter		Jude	
Titus		1:2	23	6	45
2:11	68	3	83	13	40
3:5	86	"	88		
		15,16	48	Revelation	
Hebrews		3:20	73	1:1	16
1:3	54	22	84	6:16	99
14	84	4:19	64	12:4	84
4:13	13	5:8	55	15:4	43
16	77			19:1	100
5:7	101	II Peter		19:1-3	87
6:16	99	2:5	34	21:27	87

This Scriptures Cited index was compiled by Miss Clara Brown, Box 22, Sopchoppy, Florida 32358, from whom other indices to Mr. Pink's works may be obtained.

THE SOLITARINESS OF GOD

The title of this article is perhaps not sufficiently explicit to indicate its theme. This is partly due to the fact that so few today are accustomed to meditate upon the personal perfections of God. Comparatively few of those who occasionally read the Bible are aware of the awe-inspiring and worship-provoking grandeur of the Divine character. That God is great in wisdom, wondrous in power, yet full of mercy, is assumed by many to be almost common knowledge; but, to entertain anything approaching an adequate conception of His being, His nature, His attributes, as these are revealed in Holy Scripture, is something which very, very few people in these degenerate times have attained unto. God is solitary in His excellency. "Who is like unto Thee, O Lord, among the gods? Who is like Thee, glorious in holiness, fearful in praises, doing wonders?" (Ex. 15:11).

"In the beginning, God" (Gen. 1:1). There was a time, if "time" it could be called, when God, in the unity of His nature (though subsisting equally in three Divine Persons), dwelt all alone. "In the beginning, God." There was no heaven, where His glory is now particularly manifested. There was no earth to engage His attention. There were no angels to hymn His praises; no universe to be upheld by the word of His power. There was nothing, no one, but God; and that, not for a day, a year, or an age, but "from ever-lasting." During a past eternity, God was alone: self-contained, self-sufficient, self-satisfied; in need of nothing. Had a universe, had angels, had human beings been necessary to Him in any way, they also had been called into existence from all eternity. The creating of them when He did, added nothing to God essentially. He changes not (Mal. 3:6), therefore His essential glory can be neither augmented nor diminished.

God was under no constraint, no obligation, no necessity to create. That He chose to do so was purely a sovereign act on His part, caused by nothing outside Himself, determined by nothing but His own mere good pleasure; for He "worketh all things after the counsel of His own will" (Eph. 1:11.) That He did create was simply for His manifestative glory. Do some of our readers imagine that we have gone beyond what Scripture warrants? Then our appeal shall be to the Law and the Testimony: "Stand up and bless the Lord your God forever and ever: and blessed be Thy glorious name, which is exalted above all blessing and praise" (Neh. 9:5). God is no gainer even from our worship. He was in no need of that external glory of His grace which arises from His redeemed, for He is glorious enough in Himself without that. What was it moved Him to predestinate His elect to the praise of the glory of His grace? It was, as Eph. 1:5 tells us, "according to the good pleasure of His will."

We are well aware that the high ground we are here treading is new and strange to almost all of our readers; for that reason it is well to move slowly. Let our appeal again be to the Scriptures. At the end of Rom. 11, where the apostle brings to a close his long argument on salvation by pure and sovereign grace, he asks, "For who hath known the mind of the Lord? Or who hath been His counsellor? Or who hath first given to Him, and it shall be recompensed to him again?" (vv. 34, 35). The force of this is, it is impossible to bring the Almighty under obligations to the creature; God gains nothing from us. "If thou be righteous, what givest thou Him? Or what receiveth He of thine hand? Thy wickedness may hurt a man as thou art; and thy righteousness may profit the son of man" (Job 35:7,8), but it certainly cannot affect God, who is all-blessed in Himself. "When ye shall have done all those things which are commanded you, say, We are unprofitable servants" (Luke 17:10)—our obedience has profited God nothing.

Nay, we go further: our Lord Jesus Christ added nothing to God in His essential being and glory, either by what He did or suffered. True, blessedly and gloriously true, He manifested the glory of God to us, but He added nought to God. He Himself expressly declares so, and there is no appeal from His words: "My goodness extendeth not to Thee" (Psa. 16:2). The whole of that Psalm is a Psalm of Christ. Christ's goodness or righteousness reached unto His saints in the earth (Psa. 16:3), but God was high above and beyond it all, God only is "the Blessed One" (Mark 14:61, Gr.).

It is perfectly true that God is both honoured and dishonoured by men; not in His essential being, but in His official character. It is equally true that God has been "glorified" by creation, by providence, and by redemption. This we do not and dare not dispute for a moment. But all of this has to do with His manifestative glory and the recognition of it by us. Yet had God so pleased He might have continued alone for all eternity, without making known His glory unto creatures. Whether He should do so or not was determined solely by His own will. He was perfectly blessed in Himself before the first creature was called into being. And what are all the creatures of His hands unto Him even now? Let Scripture again make answer:

"Behold, the nations are as a drop of a bucket, and are

counted as the small dust of the balance: behold, He taketh up the isles as a very little thing. And Lebanon is not sufficient to burn, nor the beasts thereof sufficient for a burnt offering. All nations before Him are as nothing; and they are counted to Him less than nothing, and vanity. To whom then will ye liken God? (Isa. 40:15-18). That is the God of Scripture; alas, He is still "the unknown God" (Acts 17:23) to the heedless multitudes. "It is He that sitteth upon the circle of the earth, and the inhabitants thereof are as grasshoppers; that stretcheth out the heavens as a curtain, and spreadeth them out as a tent to dwell in: that bringeth the princes to nothing; He maketh the judges of the earth as vanity" (Isa. 40:22,23). How vastly different is the God of Scripture from the "god" of the average pulpit!

Nor is the testimony of the New Testament any different from that of the Old: how could it be, seeing that both have one and the same Author! There too we read, "Which in His times He shall show, who is the blessed and only Potentate, the King of kings, and Lord of lords: Who only hath immortality, dwelling in the light which no man can approach unto; whom no man hath seen, nor can see: to whom be honour and power everlasting, Amen" (I Tim. 6:16). Such a One is to be revered, worshipped, adored. He is solitary in His majesty, unique in His excellency, peerless in His perfections. He sustains all, but is Himself independent of all. He gives to all, but is enriched by none.

Such a God cannot be found out by searching; He can be known, only as He is revealed to the heart by the Holy Spirit through the Word. It is true that creation demonstrates a Creator, and that, so plainly, men are "without excuse"; yet, we still have to say with Job, "Lo, these are parts of His ways: but how little a portion is heard of Him?

4

but the thunder of His power who can understand?" (26: 14). The so-called argument from design by well-meaning "Apologists" has, we believe, done much more harm than good, for it has attempted to bring down the great God to the level of finite comprehension, and thereby has lost sight of His solitary excellence.

Analogy has been drawn between a savage finding a watch upon the sands, and from a close examination of it he infers a watch-maker. So far so good. But attempt to go further: Suppose that savage sits down on the sand and endeavors to form to himself a conception of this watch-maker, his personal affections and manners; his disposition, acquirements, and moral character—all that goes to make up a personality; could he ever think or reason out a real man—the man who made the watch, so that he could say, "I am acquainted with him"? It seems trifling to ask such questions, but is the eternal and infinite God so much more within the grasp of human reason? No, indeed. The God of Scripture can only be known by those to whom He makes Himself known.

Nor is God known by the intellect. "God is Spirit" (John 4:24), and therefore can only be known spiritually. But fallen man is not spiritual, he is carnal. He is dead to all that is spiritual. Unless he is born again, supernaturally brought from death unto life, miraculously translated out of darkness into light, he cannot even see the things of God (John 3:3), still less apprehend them (I Cor. 2:14). The Holy Spirit has to shine in our hearts (not intellects) in order to give us "the knowledge of the glory of God in the face of Jesus" (II Cor. 4:6). And even that spiritual knowledge is but fragmentary. The regenerated soul has to grow in grace and in the knowledge of the Lord Jesus (II Pet. 3:18).

5

The principal prayer and aim of Christians should be that we "walk worthy of the Lord unto all pleasing, being fruitful in every good work and increasing in the knowledge of God" (Col. 1:10).

THE DECREES OF GOD

The decree of God is His purpose or determination with respect to future things. We have used the singular number as Scripture does (Rom. 8:28, Eph. 3:11), because there was only one act of His infinite mind about future things. But we speak as if there had been many, because our minds are only capable of thinking of successive revolutions, as thoughts and occasions arise, or in reference to the various objects of His decree, which being many seem to us to require a distinct purpose for each one. But an infinite understanding does not proceed by steps, from one stage to another: "Known unto God are all His works, from the beginning of the world" (Acts 15:18).

The Scriptures make mention of the decrees of God in many passages, and under a variety of terms. The word "decree" is found in Psa. 2:7, etc. In Eph. 3:11 we read of His "eternal purpose." In Acts 2:23 of His "determinate counsel and foreknowledge." In Eph. 1:9 of the mystery of His "will." In Rom. 8:29 that He also did "predestinate." In Eph. 1:9 of His "good pleasure." God's decrees are called His "counsel" to signify they are consummately wise. They are called God's "will" to show He was under no control, but acted according to His own pleasure. When a man's will is the rule of his conduct, it is usually capricious and unreasonable; but wisdom is always associated with "will" in the Divine proceedings, and accordingly, God's decrees are said to be "the counsel of His own will" (Eph. 1:11).

The decrees of God relate to all future things without exception; whatever is done in time, was foreordained before time began. God's purpose was concerned with everything, whether great or small, whether good or evil, although with reference to the latter we must be careful to state that while God is the Orderer and Controller of sin, He is not the Author of it in the same way that He is the Author of good. Sin could not proceed from a holy God by positive and direct creation, but only by decretive permission and negative action. God's decree is as comprehensive as His government, extending to all creatures and all events. It was concerned about our life and death; about our state in time, and our state in eternity. As God works all things after the counsel of His own will, we learn from His works what His counsel is (was), as we judge of an architect's plan by inspecting the building which was erected under his directions.

God did not merely decree to make man, place him upon the earth, and then leave him to his own uncontrolled guidance; instead, He fixed all the circumstances in the lot of individuals, and all the particulars which will comprise the history of the human race from its commencement to its close. He did not merely decree that general laws should be established for the government of the world, but He settled the application of those laws to all particular cases. Our days are numbered, and so are the hairs of our heads. We may learn what is the extent of the Divine decrees from the dispensations of providence, in which they are executed. The care of Providence reaches to the most insignificant creatures, and the most minute events—the death of a sparrow, and the fall of a hair.

Let us now consider some of the properties of the Di-

8

vine decrees. First, they are eternal. To suppose any of them to be made in time, is to suppose that some new occasion has occurred, some unforeseen event or combination of circumstances has arisen, which has induced the Most High to form a new resolution. This would argue that the knowledge of the Deity is limited, and that He is growing wiser in the progress of time—which would be horrible blasphemy. No man who believes that the Divine understanding is infinite, comprehending the past, the present, and the future, will ever assent to the erroneous doctrine of temporal decrees. God is not ignorant of future events which will be executed by human volitions; He has foretold them in innumerable instances, and prophecy is but the manifestation of His eternal prescience. Scripture affirms that believers were chosen in Christ before the world began (Eph. 1:4), yea, that grace was "given" to them then (II Tim. 1:9).

Second, the decrees of God are wise. Wisdom is shown in the selection of the best possible ends and of the fittest means of accomplishing them. That this character belongs to the decrees of God is evident from what we know of them. They are disclosed to us by their execution, and every proof of wisdom in the works of God is a proof of the wisdom of the plan, in conformity to which they are performed. As the Psalmist declared, "O Lord, how manifold are Thy works! in wisdom hast Thou made them all" (Psalm 104:24). It is indeed but a very small part of them which falls under our observation, yet, we ought to proceed here as we do in other cases, and judge of the whole by the specimen, of what is unknown, by what is known. He who perceives the workings of admirable skill in the parts of a machine which he has an opportunity to examine, is naturally led to believe that the other parts are equally admirable. In like manner should we satisfy

9

our minds as to God's works when doubts obtrude themselves upon us, and repel the objections which may be suggested by something which we cannot reconcile to our notions of what is good and wise. When we reach the bounds of the finite and gaze toward the mysterious realm of the infinite, let us exclaim, "O the depth of the riches! both of the wisdom and knowledge of God" (Rom. 11:33).

Third, they are free. "Who hath directed the Spirit of the Lord, or being His counsellor hath taught Him? With whom took He counsel, and who instructed Him, and taught Him in the path of judgment, and taught Him knowledge, and showed to Him the way of understanding?" (Isa. 40:13,14). God was alone when He made His decrees, and His determinations were influenced by no external cause. He was free to decree or not to decree, and to decree one thing and not another. This liberty we must ascribe to Him who is supreme, independent, and sovereign in all His doings.

Fourth, they are absolute and unconditional. The execution of them is not suspended upon any condition which may, or may not be, performed. In every instance where God has decreed an end, He has also decreed every means to that end. The One who decreed the salvation of His elect also decreed to work faith in them (II Thess. 2:13). "My counsel shall stand, and I will do all My pleasure" (Isa. 46:10): but that could not be, if His counsel depended upon a condition which might not be performed. But God "worketh all things after the counsel of His own will" (Eph. 1:11).

Side by side with the immutability and invincibility of God's decrees, Scripture plainly teaches that man is a responsible creature and answerable for his actions. And if our thoughts are formed from God's Word the maintenance of the one wll not lead to the denial of the other.

That there is a real difficulty in defining where the one ends and the other begins, is freely granted. This is ever the case where there is a conjunction of the Divine and the human. Real prayer is indited by the Spirit, yet it is also the cry of a human heart. The Scriptures are the inspired Word of God, yet were they written by men who were something more than machines in the hand of the Spirit. Christ is both God and man. He is Omniscient, yet "increased in wisdom" (Luke 2:52). He was Almighty, yet was "crucified through weakness" (II Cor. 13:4). He was the Prince of life, yet He died. High mysteries are these, yet faith receives them unquestioningly.

It has often been pointed out in the past that every objection made against the eternal decrees of God applies with equal force against His eternal foreknowledge. "Whether God has decreed all things that ever come to pass or not, all that own the being of a God, own that He knows all things beforehand. Now, it is self-evident that if He knows all things beforehand, He either doth approve of them or doth not approve of them; that is, He either is willing they should be, or He is not willing they should be. But to will that they should be is to decree them" (Jonathan Edwards).

Finally, attempt to assume and then contemplate the opposite. To deny the Divine decrees would be to predicate a world and all its concerns regulated by un-designed chance or blind fate. Then what peace, what assurance, what comfort would there be for our poor hearts and minds? What refuge would there be to fly to in the hour of need and trial? None at all. There would be nothing better than the black darkness and abject horror of atheism. O my reader, how thankful should we be that everything is determined by infinite wisdom and goodness! What praise and gratitude are due unto God for His Divine decrees. It is because of them that "we know that all things work together for good to them that love God, to them who are the called according to His purpose" (Rom. 8:28). Well may we exclaim, "For of Him, and through Him, and to Him, are all things: to whom be glory forever. Amen" (Rom. 11:36).

THE KNOWLEDGE OF GOD

God is omniscient. He knows everything: everything possible, everything actual; all events, all creatures, of the past, the present and the future. He is perfectly acquainted with every detail in the life of every being in heaven, in earth and in hell. "He knoweth what is in the darkness" (Dan. 2:22). Nothing escapes His notice, nothing can be hidden from Him, nothing is forgotten by Him. Well may we say with the Psalmist, "Such knowledge is too wonderful for me; it is high, I cannot attain unto it" (Psa. 139:6). His knowledge is perfect. He never errs, never changes, never overlooks anything. "Neither is there any creature that is not manifest in His sight: but all things are naked and opened unto the eyes of Him with whom we have to do" (Heb. 4:13). Yes, such is the God with whom we "have to do"!

"Thou knowest my downsitting and mine uprising, Thou understandest my thoughts afar off. Thou compassest my path and my lying down, and art acquainted with all my ways. For there is not a word in my tongue but, lo, O Lord, Thou knowest it altogether" (Psa. 139:2-4). What a wondrous Being is the God of Scripture! Each of His glorious attributes should render Him honourable in our esteem. The apprehension of His omniscience ought to bow us in adoration before Him. Yet how little do we meditate upon this Divine perfection! Is it because the very thought of it fills us with uneasiness?

How solemn is this fact: nothing can be concealed from God! "For I know the things that come into your mind, every one of them" (Ezek. 11:5). Though He be invisible to us, we are not so to Him. Neither the darkness of night, the closest curtains, nor the deepest dungeon can hide any sinner from the eyes of Omniscience. The trees of the garden were not able to conceal our first parents. No human eye beheld Cain murder his brother, but his Maker witnessed his crime. Sarah might laugh derisively in the seclusion of her tent, yet was it heard by Jehovah. Achan stole a wedge of gold and carefully hid it in the earth, but God brought it to light. David was at much pains to cover up his wickedness, but ere long the all-seeing God sent one of His servants to say to him, "Thou art the man!" And to writer and reader is also said, "Be sure your sin will find you out" (Num. 32:23).

Men would strip Deity of His omniscience it they could—what a proof that "the carnal mind is enmity against God" (Rom. 8:7)! The wicked do as naturally hate this Divine perfection as much as they are naturally compelled to acknowledge it. They wish there might be no Witness of their sins, no Searcher of their hearts, no Judge of their deeds. They seek to banish such a God from their thoughts: "They consider not in their hearts that I remember all their wickedness" (Hosea 7:2). How solemn is Psa. 90:8! Good reason has every Christ-rejecter for trembling before it: "Thou hast set our iniquities before Thee, our secret sins in the light of Thy countenance."

But to the believer, the fact of God's omniscience is a truth fraught with much comfort. In times of perplexity he says with Job, "But He knoweth the way that I take" (23:10). It may be profoundly mysterious to me, quite incomprehensible to my friends, but "He knoweth"! In times of weariness and weakness believers assure themselves "He knoweth our frame; He remembereth that we are dust" (Psa. 103:14). In times of doubt and suspicion they appeal to this very attribute, saying, "Search me, O God, and know my heart: try me, and know my thoughts: and see if there be any wicked way in me, and lead me in the way everlasting" (Psa. 139:23,24). In time of sad failure, when our actions have belied our hearts, when our deeds have repudiated our devotion, and the searching question comes to us, "Lovest thou Me?"; we say, as Peter did, "Lord, Thou knowest all things; Thou knowest that I love Thee" (John 21:17).

Here is encouragement to prayer. There is no cause for fearing that the petitions of the righteous will not be heard, or that their sighs and tears shall escape the notice of God since He knows the thoughts and intents of the heart. There is no danger of the individual saint being overlooked amidst the multitude of supplicants who daily and hourly present their various petitions, for an infinite Mind is as capable of paying the same attention to millions as if only one individual were seeking its attention. So too the lack of appropriate language, the inability to give expression to the deepest longing of the soul, will not jeopardize our prayers, for "It shall come to pass, that before they call, I will answer; and while they are yet speaking, I will hear" (Isa. 65:24).

"Great is our Lord, and of great power: His understanding is infinite" (Psa. 147:5). God not only knows whatsoever has happened in the past in every part of His vast domains, and He is not only thoroughly acquainted with everything that is now transpiring throughout the entire universe, but He is also perfectly cognizant with every event, from the least to the greatest, that ever will happen in the ages to come. God's knowledge of the future is as complete as is His knowledge of the past and the present, and that, because the future depends entirely upon Himself. Were it in anywise possible for something to occur apart from either the direct agency or permission of God, then that something would be independent of Him, and He would at once cease to be Supreme.

Now the Divine knowledge of the future is not a mere abstraction, but something which is inseparably connected with and accompanied by His purpose. God has Himself designed whatsoever shall yet be, and what He has designed must be effectuated. As His most sure Word affirms, "He doeth according to His will in the army of heaven, and among the inhabitants of the earth: and none can stay His hand" (Dan. 4:35). And again, "There are many devices in a man's heart; nevertheless the counsel of the Lord, that shall stand" (Prov. 19:21). The wisdom and power of God being alike infinite, the accomplishment of whatever He hath purposed is absolutely guaranteed. It is no more possible for the Divine counsels to fail in their execution than it would be for the thrice holy God to lie.

Nothing relating to the future is in anywise uncertain so far as the actualization of God's counsels are concerned. None of His decrees are left contingent either on creatures or secondary causes. There is no future event which is only a mere possibility, that is, something which may or may not come to pass, "Known unto God are all His works from the beginning" (Acts 15:18). Whatever God has decreed is inexorably certain, for He is without variableness, or shadow of turning (James 1:17). Therefore we are told at the very beginning of that book which unveils to us so much of the future, of "Things which must shortly come to pass" (Rev. 1:1).

The perfect knowledge of God is exemplified and illustrated in every prophecy recorded in His Word. In the O. T. are to be found scores of predictions concerning the

16

history of Israel, which were fulfilled to their minutest detail, centuries after they were made. In them too are scores more foretelling the earthly career of Christ, and they too were accomplished literally and perfectly. Such prophecies could only have been given by One who knew the end from the beginning, and whose knowledge rested upon the unconditional certainty of the accomplishment of everything foretold. In like manner, both Old and New Testament contain many other announcements yet future, and they too "must be fulfilled" (Luke 24:44), must because foretold by Him who decreed them.

It should, however, be pointed out that neither God's knowledge nor His cognition of the future, considered simply in themselves, are causative. Nothing has ever come to pass, or ever will, merely because God knew it. The cause of all things is the will of God. The man who really believes the Scriptures knows beforehand that the seasons will continue to follow each other with unfailing regularity to the end of earth's history (Gen.8:22), yet his knowledge is not the cause of their succession. So God's knowledge does not arise from things because they are or will be, but because He has ordained them to be. God knew and foretold the crucifixion of His Son many hundreds of years before He became incarnate, and this, because in the Divine purpose, He was a Lamb slain from the foundation of the world: hence we read of His being "delivered by the determinate counsel and foreknowledge of God" (Acts 2:23).

A word or two by way of application. The infinite knowledge of God should fill us with amazement. How far exalted above the wisest man is the Lord! None of us knows what a day may bring forth, but all futurity is open to His omniscient gaze. The infinite knowledge of God ought to fill us with holy awe. Nothing we do, say, or even think, escapes the cognizance of Him with whom we have to do: "The eyes of the Lord are in every place, beholding the evil and the good" (Prov. 15:3). What a curb this would be unto us, did we but meditate upon it more frequently! Instead of acting recklessly, we should say with Hagar, "Thou God seest me" (Gen. 16:13). The apprehension of God's infinite knowledge should fill the Christian with adoration. The whole of my life stood open to His view from the beginning. He foresaw my every fall, my every sin, my every backsliding; yet, nevertheless, fixed His heart upon me. Oh, how the realization of this should bow me in wonder and worship before Him!

THE FOREKNOWLEDGE OF GOD

What controversies have been engendered by this subject in the past! But what truth of Holy Scripture is there which has not been made the occasion of theological and ecclesiastical battles? The deity of Christ, His virgin birth, His atoning death, His second advent; the believer's justification, sanctification, security; the church, its organization, officers, discipline; baptism, the Lord's supper, and a score of other precious truths might be mentioned. Yet, the controversies which have been waged over them did not close the mouths of God's faithful servants; why, then, should we avoid the vexing question of God's Foreknowledge, because, forsooth, there are some who will charge us with fomenting strife? Let others contend if they will, our duty is to bear witness according to the light vouchsafed us.

There are two things concerning the Foreknowledge of God about which many are in ignorance: the meaning of the term, its Scriptural scope. Because this ignorance is so widespread, it is an easy matter for preachers and teachers to palm off perversions of this subject, even upon the people of God. There is only one safeguard against error, and that is to be established in the faith; and for that, there has to be prayerful and diligent study, and a receiving with meekness the engrafted Word of God. Only then are we fortified against the attacks of those who assail us. There are those today who are mis-using this very truth in order to discredit and deny the absolute sovereignty of God in the salvation of sinners. Just as higher critics are repudiating the Divine inspiration of the Scriptures; evolutionists, the work of God in creation; so some pseudo Bible teachers are perverting His foreknowledge in order to set aside His unconditional election unto eternal life.

When the solemn and blessed subject of Divine foreordination is expounded, when God's eternal choice of certain ones to be conformed to the image of His Son is set forth, the Enemy sends along some man to argue that election is based upon the foreknowledge of God, and this "foreknowledge" is interpreted to mean that God foresaw certain ones would be more pliable than others, that they would respond more readily to the strivings of the Spirit, and that because God knew they would believe, He, accordingly, predestinated them unto salvation. But such a statement is radically wrong. It repudiates the truth of total depravity, for it argues that there is something good in some men. It takes away the independency of God, for it makes His decrees rest upon what He discovers in the creature. It completely turns things upside down, for in saying God foresaw certain sinners would believe in Christ, and that because of this, He predestinated them unto salvation, is the very reverse of the truth. Scripture affirms that God, in His high sovereignty, singled out certain ones to be recipients of His distinguishing favours (Acts 13:48), and therefore He determined to bestow upon them the gift of faith. False theology makes God's foreknowledge of our believing the cause of His election to salvation; whereas, God's election is the cause, and our believing in Christ is the effect.

Ere proceeding further with our discussion of this much misunderstood theme, let us pause and define our terms. What is meant by "foreknowledge"? "To know before-

20

hand," is the ready reply of many. But we must not jump at conclusions, nor must we turn to Webster's dictionary as the final court of appeal, for it is not a matter of the etymology of the term employed. What is needed is to find out how the word is used in Scripture. The Holy Spirit's usage of an expression always defines its meaning and scope. It is failure to apply this simple rule which is responsible for so much confusion and error. So many people assume they already know the signification of a certain word used in Scripture, and then they are too dilatory to test their assumptions by means of a concordance. Let us amplify this point.

Take the word "flesh." Its meaning appears to be so obvious that many would regard it as a waste of time to look up its various connections in Scripture. It is hastily assumed that the word is synonymous with the physical body, and so no inquiry is made. But, in fact, "flesh" in Scripture frequently includes far more than what is corporeal; all that is embraced by the term can only be ascertained by a diligent comparison of every occurrence of it and by a study of each separate context. Take the word "world." The average reader of the Bible imagines this word is the equivalent for the human race, and consequently, many passages where the term is found are wrongly interpreted. Take the word "immortality." Surely it requires no study! Obviously it has reference to the indestructibility of the soul. Ah, my reader, it is foolish and wrong to assume anything where the Word of God is concerned. If the reader will take the trouble to carefully examine each passage where "mortal" and "immortal" are found, it will be seen these words are never applied to the soul, but always to the body.

Now what has just been said on "flesh," the "world," "immortality," applies with equal force to the terms "know" and "foreknow." Instead of imagining that these words signify no more than a simple cognition, the different passages in which they occur require to be carefully weighed. The word "foreknowledge" is not found in the Old Testament. But "know" occurs there frequently. When that term is used in connection with God, it often signifies to regard with favour, denoting not mere cognition but an affection for the object in view. "I know thee by name" (Ex. 33:17). "Ye have been rebellious against the Lord from the day that I knew you" (Deut. 9:24). "Before I formed thee in the belly I knew thee" (Jer. 1:5). "They have made princes and I knew not" (Hos. 8:4). "You only have I known of all the families of the earth" (Amos 3:2). In these passages "knew" signifies either loved or appointed.

In like manner, the word "know" is frequently used in the New Testament, in the same sense as in the Old Testament. "Then will I profess unto them, I never knew you" (Matt. 7:23). "I am the good shepherd and know My sheep and am known of Mine" (John 10:14). "If any man love God, the same is known of Him" (I Cor. 8:3). "The Lord knoweth them that are His" (II Tim. 2:19).

Now the word "foreknowledge" as it is used in the N. T. is less ambiguous than in its simple form "to know." If every passage in which it occurs is carefully studied, it will be discovered that it is a moot point whether it ever has reference to the mere perception of events which are yet to take place. The fact is that "foreknowledge" is never used in Scripture in connection with events or actions; instead, it always has reference to persons. It is persons God is said to "foreknow," not the actions of those persons. In proof of this we shall now quote each passage where this expression is found.

The first occurrence is in Acts 2:23. There we read,

"Him being delivered by the determinate counsel and fore-knowledge of God, ye have taken, and by wicked hands have crucified and slain." If careful attention is paid to the wording of this verse it will be seen that the apostle was not there speaking of God's foreknowledge of the act of the crucifixion, but of the Person crucified: "Him (Christ) being delivered by," etc.

The second occurrence is in Rom. 8:29,30. "For whom He did foreknow, He also did predestinate to be conformed to the image of His Son, that He might be the Firstborn among many brethren. Moreover whom He did predesti-nate, them He also called," etc. Weigh well the pronoun that is used here. It is not what He did foreknow, but whom He did. It is not the surrendering of their wills nor the believing of their hearts, but the persons them-selves, which is here in view.

"God hath not cast away His people which He fore-knew" (Rom. 11:2). Once more the plain reference is to persons, and to persons only.

The last mention is in I Peter 1:2: "Elect according to the foreknowledge of God the Father." Who are "elect according to the foreknowledge of God the Father"? The previous verse tells us: the reference is to the "strangers scattered," i. e., the Diaspora, the Dispersion, the believing Jews. Thus, here too the reference is to persons, and not to their foreseen acts.

Now in view of these passages (and there are no more) what scriptural ground is there for anyone saying God "foreknew" the acts of certain ones, viz., their "repenting and believing," and that because of those acts He elected them unto salvation? The answer is, None whatever. Scripture never speaks of repentance and faith as being foreseen or foreknown by God. Truly, He did know from all eternity that certain ones would repent and believe, yet this is not what Scripture refers to as the object of God's "foreknowledge." The word uniformly refers to God's foreknowing persons; then let us "hold fast the form of sound words" (II Tim. 1:13).

Another thing to which we desire to call particular attention is that the first two passages quoted above show plainly and teach implicitly that God's "foreknowledge" is not causative, that instead, something else lies behind, precedes it, and that something is His own sovereign decree. Christ was "delivered by the (1) determinate counsel and (2) foreknowledge of God" (Acts 2:23). His "counsel" or decree was the ground of His foreknowledge. So again in Rom. 8:29. That verse opens with the word "for," which tells us to look back to what immediately preceeds. What, then, does the previous verse say? This, "all things work together for good to them . . . who are the called according to His purpose." Thus God's "foreknowledge" is based upon His "purpose" or decree (see Psa. 2:7).

God foreknows what will be because He has decreed what shall be. It is therefore a reversing of the order of Scripture, a putting of the cart before the horse, to affirm that God elects because He foreknows people. The truth is, He "foreknows" because He has elected. This removes the ground or cause of election from outside the creature, and places it in God's own sovereign will. God purposed in Himself to elect a certain people, not because of anything good in them or from them, either actual or foreseen, but solely out of His own mere pleasure. As to why He chose the ones He did, we do not know, and can only say, "Even so, Father, for so it seemed good in Thy sight." The plain truth of Rom. 8:29 is that God, before the foundation of the world, singled out certain sinners and appointed them unto salvation (II Thess. 2:13). This is clear from the concluding words of the verse: "Predestinated to be conformed to the image of His son," etc. God did not predestinate those whom He foreknew were "conformed," but, on the contrary, those whom He "foreknew" (i. e., loved and elected) He predestinated "to be conformed." Their conformity to Christ is not the cause, but the effect of God's foreknowledge and predestination.

God did not elect any sinner because He foresaw that he would believe, for the simple but sufficient reason that no sinner ever does believe until God gives him faith; just as no man sees until God gives him sight. Sight is God's gift, seeing is the consequence of my using His gift. So faith is God's gift (Eph. 2:8,9), believing is the consequence of my using His gift. If it were true that God had elected certain ones to be saved because in due time they would believe, then that would make believing a meritorious act, and in that event the saved sinner would have ground for "boasting," which Scripture emphatically denies: Eph. 2:9.

Surely God's Word is plain enough in teaching that believing is not a meritorious act. It affirms that Christians are a people "who have believed through grace" (Acts 18:27). If, then, they have believed "through grace," there is absolutely nothing meritorious about "believing," and if nothing meritorious, it could not be the ground or cause which moved. God to choose them. No; God's choice proceeds not from anything in us, or anything from us, but solely from His own sovereign pleasure. Once more, in Rom. 11:5, we read of "a remnant according to the election of grace." There it is, plain enough; election itself is of grace, and grace is unmerited favour, something for which we had no claim upon God whatsoever.

It thus appears that it is highly important for us to have clear and scriptural views of the "foreknowledge" of God. Erroneous conceptions about it lead inevitably to thoughts most dishonouring to Him. The popular idea of Divine foreknowledge is altogether inadequate. God not only knew the end from the beginning, but He planned, fixed, predestinated everything from the beginning. And, as cause stands to effect, so God's purpose is the ground of His prescience. If then the reader be a real Christian, he is so because God chose him in Christ before the foundation of the world (Eph. 1:4), and chose not because He foresaw you would believe, but chose simply because it pleased Him to choose; chose you notwithstanding your natural unbelief. This being so, all the glory and praise belongs alone to Him. You have no ground for taking any credit to yourself. You have "believed through grace" (Acts 18:27), and that, because your very election was "of grace" (Rom. 11:5).

THE SUPREMACY OF GOD

In one of his letters to Erasmus, Luther said, "Your thoughts of God are too human." Probably that renowned scholar resented such a rebuke, the more so, since it proceeded from a miner's son: nevertheless, it was thoroughly deserved. We too, though having no standing among the religious leaders of this degenerate age, prefer the same charge against the majority of the preachers of our day, and against those who, instead of searching the Scriptures for themselves, lazily accept the teaching of others. The most dishonoring and degrading conceptions of the rule and reign of the Almighty are now held almost everywhere. To countless thousands, even among those professing to be Christians, the God of the Scriptures is quite unknown.

Of old, God complained to an apostate Israel, "Thou thoughtest that I was altogether as thyself" (Psa. 50:21). Such must now be His indictment against an apostate Christendom. Men imagine that the Most High is moved by sentiment, rather than actuated by principle. They suppose that His omnipotency is such an idle fiction that Satan is thwarting His designs on every side. They think that if He has formed any plan or purpose at all, then it must be like theirs, constantly subject to change. They openly declare that whatever power He possesses must be restricted, lest He invade the citadel of man's "free will" and reduce him to a "machine." They lower the all-efficacious Atonement, which has actually redeemed everyone

27

for whom it was made, to a mere "remedy," which sin-sick souls may use if they feel disposed to; and they enervate the invincible work of the Holy Spirit to an "offer" of the Gospel which sinners may accept or reject as they please.

The "god" of this twentieth century no more resembles the Supreme Sovereign of Holy Writ than does the dim flickering of a candle the glory of the midday sun. The "god" who is now talked about in the average pulpit, spoken of in the ordinary Sunday School, mentioned in much of the religious literature of the day, and preached in most of the so-called Bible Conferences is the figment of human imagination, an invention of maudlin sentimentality. The heathen outside of the pale of Christendom form "gods" out of wood and stone, while the millions of heathen inside Christendom manufacture a "god" out of their own carnal mind. In reality, they are but atheists, for there is no other possible alternative between an absolutely supreme God, and no God at all. A "god" whose will is resisted, whose designs are frustrated, whose purpose is checkmated, possesses no title to Deity, and so far from being a fit object of worship, merits nought but contempt.

The supremacy of the true and living God might well be argued from the infinite distance which separates the mightiest creatures from the almighty Creator. He is the Potter, they are but the clay in His hands, to be moulded into vessels of honour, or to be dashed into pieces (Psa. 2:9) as He pleases. Were all the denizens of heaven and all the inhabitants of the earth to combine in revolt against Him, it would occasion Him no uneasiness, and would have less effect upon His eternal and unassailable Throne than has the spray of Mediterranian's waves upon the towering rocks of Gibraltar. So puerile and powerless is the creature to affect the Most High, Scripture itself tells us that when the Gentile heads unite with apostate Israel to defy Jehovah and His Christ, "He that sitteth in the heavens shall laugh" (Psa. 2:4).

The absolute and universal supremacy of God is plainly and positively affirmed in many scriptures. "Thine, O Lord, is the greatness, and the power, and the glory, and the victory and the majesty: for all in the heaven and all in the earth is Thine; Thine is the Kingdom, O Lord, and Thou art exalted as Head above all . . . And Thou reignest over all" (I Chron. 29:11,12)—note, "reignest" now, not "will do so in the Millennium." "O Lord God of our fathers, art not Thou God in heaven? and rulest not Thou over all the kingdoms of the heathen? and in Thine hand is there not power and might, so that none (not even the Devil himself) is able to withstand Thee?" (II Chron. 20:6). Before Him presidents and popes, kings and emperors, are less than grasshoppers.

"But He is in one mind, and who can turn Him? and what His soul desireth, even that He doeth" (Job 23:13). Ah, my reader, the God of Scripture is no make-believe monarch, no mere imaginary sovereign, but King of kings, and Lord of lords. "I know that Thou canst do everything, and that no thought of Thine can be hindered" (Job 42:3, margin), or, as another translator, "no purpose of Thine can be frustrated." All that He has designed He does. All that He has decreed, He performs. "But our God is in the heavens: He hath done whatsoever He hath pleased" (Psa. 115:3); and why has He? Because "there is no wisdom, nor understanding, nor counsel against the Lord" (Prov. 21:30).

God's supremacy over the works of His hands is vividly depicted in Scripture. Inanimate matter, irrational creatures, all perform their Maker's bidding. At His pleasure the Red Sea divided and its waters stood up as walls (Ex. 14); and the earth opened her mouth, and guilty rebels went down alive into the pit (Num. 14). When He so ordered, the sun stood still (Josh. 10); and on another occasion went backward ten degrees on the dial of Ahaz (Isa. 38:8). To exemplify His supremacy, He made ravens carry food to Elijah (I Kings 17), iron to swim on top of the waters (II Kings 6:5), lions to be tame when Daniel was cast into their den, fire to burn not when the three Hebrews were flung into its flames. Thus "Whatsoever the Lord pleased, that did He in heaven, and in earth, in the seas, and all deep places" (Psa. 135:6).

God's supremacy is also demonstrated in His perfect rule over the wills of men. Let the reader ponder carefully Ex. 34:24. Three times in the year all the males of Israel were required to leave their homes and go up to Jerusalem. They lived in the midst of hostile people, who hated them for having appropriated their lands. What, then, was to hinder the Canaanites from seizing their opportunity, and, during the absence of the men, slaying the women and children and taking possession of their farms? If the hand of the Almighty was not upon the wills even of wicked men, how could He make this promise beforehand, that none should so much as "desire" their lands? Ah, "The king's heart is in the hand of the Lord, as the rivers of water: He turneth it whithersoever He will" (Prov. 21:1).

But, it may be objected, do we not read again and again in Scripture how that men defied God, resisted His will, broke His commandments, disregarded His warnings, and turned a deaf ear to all His exhortations? Certainly we do. And does this nullify all that we have said above? If it does, then the Bible plainly contradicts itself. But that cannot be. What the objector refers to is simply the wickedness of man against the external word of God, whereas what we have mentioned above is what God has purposed in Himself. The rule of conduct He has given us to walk by, is perfectly fulfilled by none of us; His own eternal "counsels" are accomplished to their minutest details.

The absolute and universal supremacy of God is affirmed with equal plainness and positiveness in the New Testament. There we are told that God "worketh all things after the counsel of His own will" (Eph. 1:11)—the Greek for "worketh" means "to work effectually." For this reason we read, "For of Him, and through Him, and to Him, are all things: to whom be glory forever. Amen" (Rom. 11:36). Men may boast that they are free agents, with a will of their own, and are at liberty to do as they please, but Scripture says to those who boast "we will go into such a city, and continue there a year, and buy and sell . . . Ye ought to say, If the Lord will" (James 4:13,15)!

Here then is a sure resting-place for the heart. Our lives are neither the product of blind fate nor the result of capricious chance, but every detail of them was ordained from all eternity, and is now ordered by the living and reigning God. Not a hair of our heads can be touched without His permission. "A man's heart deviseth his way: but the Lord directeth his steps" (Prov. 16:9). What assurance, what strength, what comfort should this give the real Christian! "My times are in Thy hand" (Psa. 31:15). Then let me "Rest in the Lord, and wait patiently for Him" (Psa. 37:7).

31

THE SOVEREIGNTY OF GOD

The sovereignty of God may be defined as the exercise of His supremacy—see preceding chapter. Being infinitely elevated above the highest creature, He is the Most High, Lord of heaven and earth. Subject to none, influenced by none, absolutely independent: God does as He pleases, only as He pleases, always as He pleases. None can thwart Him, none can hinder Him. So His own Word expressly declares: "My counsel shall stand, and I will do all My pleasure" (Isa. 46:10); "He doeth according to His will in the army of heaven, and the inhabitants of the earth: and none can stay His hand" (Dan. 4:35). Divine sovereignty means that God is God in fact, as well as in name, that He is on the Throne of the universe, directing all things, working all things "after the counsel of His own will" (Eph. 1:11).

Rightly did the late Mr. Spurgeon say in his sermon on Matt. 20:15, "There is no attribute more comforting to His children than that of God's Sovereignty. Under the most adverse circumstances, in the most severe trials, they believe that Sovereignty has ordained their afflictions, that Sovereignty overrules them, and that Sovereignty will sanctify them all. There is nothing for which the children ought more earnestly to contend than the doctrine of their Master over all creation—the Kingship of God over all the works of His own hands—the Throne of God and His right to sit upon that Throne. On the other hand, there is no doctrine more hated by worldings, no truth of which they have made such a football, as the great, stupendous, but yet most certain doctrine of the Sovereignty of the infinite Jehovah. Men will allow God to be everywhere except on His throne. They will allow Him to be in His workshop to fashion worlds and make stars. They will allow Him to be in His almonry to dispense His alms and bestow His bounties. They will allow Him to sustain the earth and bear up the pillars thereof, or light the lamps of heaven, or rule the waves of the ever-moving ocean; but when God ascends His throne, His creatures then gnash their teeth, and we proclaim an enthroned God, and His right to do as He wills with His own, to dispose of His creatures as He thinks well, without consulting them in the matter; then it is that we are hissed and execrated, and then it is that men turn a deaf ear to us, for God on His throne is not the God they love. But it is God upon the throne that we love to preach. It is God upon His throne whom we trust."

"Whatsoever the Lord pleased, that did He in heaven, and in earth, in the seas, and all deep places" (Psa.135:6). Yes, dear reader, such is the imperial Potentate revealed in Holy Writ. Unrivalled in majesty, unlimited in power, unaffected by anything outside Himself. But we are living in a day when even the most "orthodox" seem afraid to admit the proper Godhood of God. They say that to press the sovereignty of God excludes human responsibility; whereas human responsibility is based upon Divine sovereignty, and is the product of it.

"But our God is in the heavens: He hath done whatsoever He hath pleased" (Psa. 115:3). He sovereignly chose to place each of His creatures on that particular footing which seemed good in His sight. He created angels: some He placed on a conditional footing, others

33

He gave an immutable standing before Him (I Tim. 5:21), making Christ their head (Col. 2:10). Let it not be overlooked that the angels which sinned (II Peter 2:5), were as much His creatures as the angels that sinned not. Yet God foresaw they would fall, nevertheless He placed them on a mutable, creature, conditional footing, and suffered them to fall, though He was not the Author of their sin.

So too, God sovereignly placed Adam in the garden of Eden upon a conditional footing. Had He so pleased, He could have placed him upon an unconditional footing; He could have placed him on a footing as firm as that occupied by the unfallen angels, He could have placed him upon a footing as sure and as immutable as that which His saints have in Christ. But, instead, He chose to set him in Eden on the basis of creature responsibility, so that he stood or fell according as he measured or failed to measure up to his responsibility—obedience to his Maker. Adam stood accountable to God by the law which his Creator had given him. Here was responsibility, unimpaired responsibility, tested out under the most favourable conditions.

Now God did not place Adam upon a footing of conditional, creature-responsibility, because it was right He should so place him. No, it was right because God did it. God did not even give creatures being because it was right for Him to do so, i. e., because He was under any obligations to create; but it was right because He did so. God is sovereign. His will is supreme. So far from God being under any law of "right," He is a law unto Himself, so that whatsoever He does is right. And woe be to the rebel that calls His sovereignty into question: "Woe unto him that striveth with his Maker. Let the potsherd strive with the potsherds of the earth. Shall the thing say to Him that fashioned it, What makest Thou?" (Isa. 45:9).

Again; the Lord God sovereignly placed Israel upon a conditional footing. The 19th, 20th, and 24th chapters of Exodus afford a clear and full proof of this. They were placed under a covenant of works. God gave to them certain laws, and made national blessing for them depend upon their observance of His statutes. But Israel were stiffnecked and uncircumcised in heart. They rebelled against Jehovah, forsook His law, turned unto false gods, apostatised. In consequence, Divine judgment fell upon them, they were delivered into the hands of their enemies, dispersed abroad throughout the earth, and remain under the heavy frown of God's displeasure to this day.

It was God in the exercise of His high sovereignty that placed Satan and his angels, Adam, Israel, in their respective responsible positions. But so far from His sovereignty taking away responsibility from the creature, it was by the exercise thereof that He placed them on this conditional footing, under such responsibilities as He thought proper; by virtue of which sovereignty, He is seen to be God over all. Thus, there is perfect harmony between the sovereignty of God and the responsibility of the creature. Many have more foolishly said that it is quite impossible to show where Divine sovereignty ends and creature accountability begins. Here is where creature responsibility begins: in the sovereign ordination of the Creator. As to His sovereignty, there is not and never will be any "end" to it!

Let us give further proofs that the responsibility of the creature is based upon God's sovereignty. How many things are recorded in Scripture which were right because God commanded them, and which would not have been right had He not so commanded! What right had Adam to "eat" of the trees of the Garden? The permission of his Maker (Gen. 2:16), without such, he had been a thief!

What right had Israel to "borrow" of the Egyptians' jewels and raiment (Ex. 12:35)? None, unless Jehovah had authorized it (Ex. 3:22). What right had Israel to slay so many lambs for sacrifice? None, except that God commanded it. What right had Israel to kill off all the Canaanites? None, save as Jehovah had bidden them. What right has the husband to require submission from his wife? None, unless God had appointed it. And so we might go on. Human responsibility is based upon Divine sovereignty.

One more example of the exercise of God's absolute sovereignty. God placed His elect upon a different footing from Adam or Israel. He placed them upon an unconditional footing. In the Everlasting Covenant Jesus Christ was appointed their Head, took their responsibilities upon Himself, and wrought out a righteousness for them which is perfect, indefeasible, eternal. Christ was placed upon a conditional footing, for He was "made under the law, to redeem them that were under the law," only with this infinite difference: the others failed, He did not and could not. And who placed Christ upon that conditional footing? The Triune God. It was sovereign will that appointed Him, sovereign love that sent Him, sovereign authority that assigned Him His work.

Certain conditions were set before the Mediator. He was to be made in the likeness of sin's flesh; He was to magnify the law and make it honorable; He was to bear all the sins of all God's people in His own body on the tree; He was to make full atonement for them; He was to endure the outpoured wrath of God; He was to die and be buried. On the fulfillment of those conditions He was promised a reward: Isa. 53:10-12. He was to be the Firstborn among many brethren; He was to have a people who should share His glory. Blessed be His name forever, He fulfilled those conditions, and because He did so, the Father stands pledged, on solemn oath, to preserve through time and bless throughout eternity every one of those for whom His incarnate Son mediated. Because He took their place, they now share His. His righteousness is theirs. His standing before God is theirs, His life is theirs. There is not a single condition for them to meet, not a single responsibility for them to discharge in order to attain their eternal bliss. "By one offering He hath perfected forever them that are set apart" (Heb. 10:14).

Here then is the sovereignty of God openly displayed before all, displayed in the different ways in which He has dealt with His creatures. Part of the angels, Adam, Israel, were placed upon a conditional footing, continuance in blessing being made dependent upon their obedience and fidelity to God. But in sharp contrast from them, the "little flock" (Luke 12:32), have been given an unconditional, an immutable standing in God's covenant, God's counsels, God's Son; their blessing being made dependent upon what Christ did for them. "The foundation of God standeth sure, having this seal: The Lord knoweth them that are His" (II Tim. 1:19). The foundation on which God's elect stand is a perfect one: nothing can be added to it, nor anything taken from it (Eccl. 3:14). Here, then, is the highest and grandest display of the absolute sovereignty of God. Verily, He has "mercy on whom He will have mercy, and whom He will He hardeneth" (Rom.9:18).

THE IMMUTABILITY OF GOD

This is one of the Divine perfections which is not suffici-ently pondered. It is one of the excellencies of the Creator which distinguishes Him from all His creatures. God is perpetually the same: subject to no change in His being, attributes, or determinations. Therefore God is compared to a rock (Deut. 32:4, etc.) which remains immovable, when the entire ocean surrounding it is continually in a fluctuating state; even so, though all creatures are subject to change, God is immutable. Because God has no be-ginning and no ending, He can know no change. He is everlastingly "the Father of lights, with whom is no variable-ness, neither shadow of turning" (James 1:17).

First, God is immutable in His essence. His nature and being are infinite, and so, subject to no mutations. There never was a time when He was not; there never will come a time when He shall cease to be. God has neither evolved, grown, nor improved. All that He is today, He has ever been, and ever will be. "I am the Lord, I change not" (Mal. 3:6) is His own unqualified affirmation. He cannot change for the better, for He is already perfect; and being perfect, He cannot change for the worse. Alto-gether unaffected by anything outside Himself, improve-ment or deterioration is impossible. He is perpetually the same. He only can say, "I am that I am" (Ex. 3:14). He is altogether uninfluenced by the flight of time. There is no wrinkle upon the brow of eternity. Therefore His power can never diminish nor His glory ever fade.

Second, God is immutable in His attributes. Whatever the attributes of God were before the universe was called into existence, they are precisely the same now, and will remain so forever. Necessarily so; for they are the very perfections, the essential qualities of His being. *Semper idem* (always the same) is written across every one of them. His power is unabated, His wisdom undiminished, His holiness unsullied. The attributes of God can no more change than Deity can cease to be. His veracity is immutable, for His Word is "forever settled in heaven" (Psa. 119:89). His love is eternal: "I have loved thee with an everlasting love" (Jer. 31:3) and "Having loved His own which were in the world, He loved them unto the end" (John 13:1). His mercy ceases not, for it is "everlasting" (Psa. 100:5).

Third, God is immutable in His counsel, His will never varies. Perhaps some are ready to object that we read "It repented the Lord that He had made man" (Gen.6:6). Our first reply is, Then do the Scriptures contradict themselves? No, that cannot be. Num. 23:19 is plain enough: "God is not a man, that He should lie; neither the son of man, that He should repent." So also in I Sam. 15:19, "The strength of Israel will not lie nor repent: for He is not a man, that He should repent." The explanation is very simple. When speaking of Himself, God frequently accommodates His language to our limited capacities. He describes Himself as clothed with bodily members, as eyes, ears, hands, etc. He speaks of Himself as "waking" (Psa. 78:65), as "rising early" (Jer. 7:13); yet He neither slumbers nor sleeps. When He institutes a change in His dealings with men, He describes His course of conduct as "repenting."

Yes, God is immutable in His counsel. "The gifts and calling of God are without repentance" (Rom. 11:29). It must be so, for "He is in one mind, and who can turn Him? and what His soul desireth, even that He doeth" (Job 23:13). Change and decay in all around we see, may He who changeth not abide with thee. God's purpose never alters. One of two things causes a man to change his mind and reverse his plans: want of foresight to anticipate everything, or lack of power to execute them. But as God is both omniscient and omnipotent there is never any need for Him to revise His decrees. No, "The counsel of the Lord standeth forever, the thoughts of His heart to all generations" (Psa. 33:11). Therefore do we read of "The immutability of His counsel" (Heb. 6:17).

Herein we may perceive the infinite distance which separates the highest creature from the Creator. Creaturehood and mutability are correlative terms. If the creature was not mutable by nature, it would not be a creature; it would be God. By nature we tend to nothing, as we came from nothing. Nothing stays our annihilation but the will and sustaining power of God. None can sustain himself a single moment. We are entirely dependent on the Creator for every breath we draw. We gladly own with the Psalmist Thou "holdest our soul in life" (Psa. 66:9). The realization of this ought to make us lie down under a sense of our own nothingness in the presence of Him "in whom we live and move, and have our being."

As fallen creatures we are not only mutable, but everything in us is opposed to God. As such we are "wandering stars" (Jude 13), out of our proper orbit. The wicked are "like the troubled sea, when it cannot rest" (Isa. 57:20). Fallen man is inconstant. The words of Jacob concerning Reuben apply with full force to all of Adam's descendants: "Unstable as water" (Gen. 49:4). Thus it is not

40

only a mark of piety, but also the part of wisdom to heed that injunction, "cease ye from man" (Isa. 2:22). No human being is to be depended on. "Put not your trust in princes, in the son of man, in whom is no help" (Psa. 146:3). If I disobey God, then I deserve to be deceived and disappointed by my fellows. People who like you today, may hate you tomorrow. The multitude who cried "Hosanna to the Son of David," speedily changed to "Away with Him, Crucify Him."

Herein is solid comfort. Human nature cannot be relied upon; but God can! However unstable I may be, however fickle my friends may prove, God changes not. If He varied as we do, if He willed one thing today and another tomorrow, if He were controlled by caprice, who could confide in Him? But, all praise to His glorious name, He is ever the same. His purpose is fixed, His will stable, His word is sure. Here then is a rock on which we may fix our feet, while the mighty torrent is sweeping away everything around us. The permanence of God's character guarantees the fulfillment of His promises: "For the mountains shall depart, and the hills be removed; but my kindness shall not depart from thee, neither shall the covenant of My peace be removed, saith the Lord that hath mercy on thee" (Isa. 54:10).

Herein is encouragement to prayer. "What comfort would it be to pray to a god that, like the chameleon, changed colour every moment? Who would put up a petition to an earthly prince that was so mutable as to grant a petition one day, and deny it another?" (S. Charnock, 1670). Should someone ask, But what is the use of praying to One whose will is already fixed? We answer, Because He so requires it. What blessings has God promised without our seeking them? "If we ask anything according to His will, He heareth us" (I John 5:14), and He has willed everything that is for His child's good. To ask for anything contrary to His will is not prayer, but rank rebellion.

Herein is terror for the wicked. Those who defy Him, break His laws, have no concern for His glory, but live their lives as though He existed not, must not suppose that, when at the last they shall cry to Him for mercy, He will alter His will, revoke His word, and rescind His awful threatenings. No, He has declared, "Therefore will I also deal in fury: Mine eye shall not spare, neither will I have pity: and though they cry in Mine ears with a loud voice, yet will I not hear them" (Ezek. 8:18). God will not deny Himself to gratify their lusts. God is holy, unchangingly so. Therefore God hates sin, eternally hates it. Hence the eternality of the punishment of all who die in their sins.

"The Divine immutability, like the cloud which interposed between the Israelites and the Egyptian army, has a dark as well as a light side. It insures the execution of His threatenings, as well as the performance of His promises; and destroys the hope which the guilty fondly cherish, that He will be all lenity to His frail and erring creatures, and that they will be much more lightly dealt with than the declarations of His own Word would lead us to expect. We oppose to these deceitful and presumptuous speculations the solemn truth, that God is unchanging in veracity and purpose, in faithfulness and justice" (J. Dick, 1850).

THE HOLINESS OF GOD

"Who shall not fear Thee, O Lord, and glorify Thy name? for Thou only art holy" (Rev. 15:4). He only is independently, infinitely, immutably holy. In Scripture He is frequently styled "The Holy One": He is so because the sum of all moral excellency is found in Him. He is absolute Purity, unsullied even by the shadow of sin. "God is light, and in Him is no darkness at all" (I John 1:5). Holiness is the very excellency of the Divine nature: the great God is "glorious in holiness" (Ex. 15:11). Therefore do we read, "Thou art of purer eyes than to behold evil, and canst not look on iniquity" (Hab. 1:13). As God's power is the opposite of the native weakness of the creature, as His wisdom is in complete contrast from the least defect of understanding or folly, so His holiness is the very antithesis of all moral blemish or defilement. Of old God appointed singers in Israel "that they should praise for the beauty of holiness" (II Chron. 20:21). "Power is God's hand or arm, omniscience His eye, mercy His bowels, eternity His duration, but holiness is His beauty" (S. Charnock). It is this, supremely, which renders Him lovely to those who are delivered from sin's dominion.

A chief emphasis is placed upon this perfection of God. "God is oftener styled Holy than Almighty, and set forth by this part of His dignity more than by any other. This is more fixed on as an epithet to His name than any other. You never find it expressed 'His mighty name' or 'His

43

wise name,' but His great name, and most of all, His holy name. This is the greatest title of honour; in this latter doth the majesty and venerableness of His name appear" (S. Charnock). This perfection, as none other, is solemnly celebrated before the Throne of Heaven, the seraphim crying, "Holy, holy, holy, is the Lord of hosts" (Isa. 6:3). God Himself singles out this perfection, "Once have I sworn by My holiness" (Psa. 89:35). God swears by His "holiness" because that is a fuller expression of Himself than anything else. Therefore we are exhorted, "Sing unto the Lord, O ye saints of His, and give thanks at the remembrance of His holiness" (Psa. 30:4). "This may be said to be a transcendental attribute, that, as it were, runs through the rest, and casts lustre upon them. It is an attribute of attributes" (J. Howe, 1670). Thus we read of "the beauty of the Lord" (Psa. 27:4), which is none other than "the beauty of holiness" (Psa. 110:3).

"As it seems to challenge an excellency above all His other perfections, so it is the glory of all the rest: as it is the glory of the Godhead, so it is the glory of every perfection in the Godhead; as His power is the strength of them, so His holiness is the beauty of them; as all would be weak without almightiness to back them, so all would be uncomely without holiness to adorn them. Should this be sullied, all the rest would lose their honour; as at the same instant the sun should lose its light, it would lose its heat, its strength, its generative and quickening virtue. As sincerity is the lustre of every grace in a Christian, so is purity the splendour of every attribute in the Godhead. His justice is a holy justice, His wisdom a holy wisdom, His power a 'holy arm' (Psa. 98:1). His truth or promise a 'holy promise' (Psa. 105:42). His name, which signifies all His attributes in conjunction, 'is holy,' Psa. 103:1" (S. Charnock).

44

God's holiness is manifested in His works. "The Lord is righteous in all His ways, and holy in all His works" (Psa. 145:17). Nothing but that which is excellent can proceed from Him. Holiness is the rule of all His actions. At the beginning He pronounced all that He made "very good" (Gen. 1:31), which He could not have done had there been anything imperfect or unholy in them. Man was made "upright" (Eccl. 7:29), in the image and likeness of his Creator. The angels that fell were created holy, for we are told that they "kept not their first habitation" (Jude 6). Of Satan it is written, "Thou wast perfect in thy ways from the day that thou wast created, till iniquity was found in thee" (Ezek. 28:15).

God's holiness is manifested in His law. That law forbids sin in all of its modifications: in its most refined as well as its grossest forms, the intent of the mind as well as the pollution of the body, the secret desire as well as the overt act. Therefore do we read, "Thy law is holy, and the commandment holy, and just, and good" (Rom. 7:12). Yes, "the commandment of the Lord is pure, enlightening the eyes. The fear of the Lord is clean, enduring forever: the judgments of the Lord are true and righteous altogether" (Psa. 19:8,9).

God's holiness is manifested at the Cross. Wondrously and yet most solemnly does the Atonement display God's infinite holiness and abhorrence of sin. How hateful must sin be to God for Him to punish it to its utmost deserts when it was imputed to His Son! "Not all the vials of judgment that have or shall be poured out upon the wicked world, nor the flaming furnace of a sinner's conscience, nor the irreversible sentence pronounced against the rebellious demons, nor the groans of the damned creatures, give such a demonstration of God's hatred of sin, as the wrath of God let loose upon His Son. Never did Divine holiness appear more beautiful and lovely than at the time our Saviour's countenance was most marred in the midst of His dying groans. This Himself acknowledges in Psa. 22. When God had turned His smiling face from Him, and thrust His sharp knife into His heart, which forced that terrible cry from Him, 'My God, My God, why hast Thou forsaken Me?' He adores this perfection—'Thou art holy,' v. 3" (S. Charnock).

Because God is holy He hates all sin. He loves everything which is in conformity to His laws, and loathes everything which is contrary to it. His Word plainly declares, "The froward is an abomination to the Lord" (Prov. 3:32). And again, "The thoughts of the wicked are an abomination to the Lord" (Prov. 15:26). It follows, therefore, that He must necessarily punish sin. Sin can no more exist without demanding His punishment than without requiring His hatred of it. God has often forgiven sinners, but He never forgives sin; and the sinner is only forgiven on the ground of Another having borne his punishment; for "without shedding of blood is no remission" (Heb. 9:22). Therefore we are told "The Lord will take vengeance on His adversaries, and He reserveth wrath for His enemies" (Nahum 1:2). For one sin God banished our first parents from Eden. For one sin all the posterity of Ham fell under a curse which remains over them to this day. For one sin Moses was excluded from Canaan, Elisha's servant smitten with leprosy, Ananias and Sapphira cut off out of the land of the living.

Herein we find proof for the Divine inspiration of the Scriptures. The unregenerate do not really believe in the holiness of God. Their conception of His character is altogether one-sided. They fondly hope that His mercy will override everything else. "Thou thoughtest that I was altogether as thyself" (Psa. 50:21) is God's charge against them. They think only of a "god" patterned after their own evil hearts. Hence their continuance in a course of mad folly. Such is the holiness ascribed to the Divine nature and character in Scripture that it clearly demonstrates their superhuman origin. The character attributed to the "gods" of the ancients and of modern heathendom are the very reverse of that immaculate purity which pertains to the true God. An ineffably holy God, who has the utmost abhorrence of all sin, was never invented by any of Adam's fallen descendants! The fact is that nothing makes more manifest the terrible depravity of man's heart and his enmity against the living God than to have set before him One who in infinitely and immutably holy. His own idea of sin is practically limited to what the world calls "crime." Anything short of that, man palliates as "defects," "mistakes," "infirmities," etc. And even where sin is owned at all, excuses and extenuations are made for it.

The "god" which the vast majority of professing Christians "love," is looked upon very much like an indulgent old man, who himself has no relish for folly, but leniently winks at the "indiscretions" of youth. But the Word says, "Thou hatest all workers of iniquity" (Psa. 5:5). And again, "God is angry with the wicked every day" (Psa. 7:11). But men refuse to believe in this God, and gnash their teeth when His hatred of sin is faithfully pressed upon their attention. No, sinful man was no more likely to devise a holy God than to create the Lake of fire in which he will be tormented for ever and ever.

Because God is holy, acceptance with Him on the ground of creature doings is utterly impossible. A fallen creature could sooner create a world than produce that which would meet the approval of infinite Purity. Can darkness dwell with Light? Can the Immaculate One take pleasure in "filthy rags" (Isa. 64:6)? The best that sinful man brings forth

47

is defiled. A corrupt tree cannot bear good fruit. God would deny Himself, vilify His perfections, were He to account as righteous and holy that which is not so in itself; and nothing is so which has the least stain upon it contrary to the nature of God. But blessed be His name, that which His holiness demanded His grace has provided in Christ Jesus our Lord. Every poor sinner who has fled to Him for refuge stands "accepted in the Beloved" (Eph. 1:6). Hallelujah!

Because God is holy the utmost reverence becomes our approaches unto Him. "God is greatly to be feared in the assembly of the saints, and to be had in reverence of all about Him" (Psa. 89:7). Then "Exalt ye the Lord our God, and worship at His footstool; He is holy" (Psa. 99:5). Yes, "At His footstool," in the lowest posture of humility, prostrate before Him. When Moses would approach unto the burning bush, God said, "put off thy shoes from off thy feet" (Ex. 3:5). He is to be served "with fear" (Psa. 2:11). Of Israel His demand was, "I will be sanctified in them that come nigh Me, and before all the people I will be glorified" (Lev. 10:3). The more our hearts are awed by His ineffable holiness, the more acceptable will be our approaches unto Him.

Because God is holy we should desire to be conformed to Him. His command is, "Be ye holy, for I am holy" (I Peter 1:16). We are not bidden to be omnipotent or omniscient as God is, but we are to be holy, and that "in all manner of deportment" (I Peter 1:15). "This is the prime way of honouring God. We do not so glorify God by elevated admirations, or eloquent expressions, or pompous services of Him, as when we aspire to a conversing with Him with unstained spirits, and live to Him in living like Him" (S. Charnock). Then as God alone is the Source and Fount of holiness, let us earnestly seek holiness from Him; let our daily prayer be that He may "sanctify us wholly; and our whole spirit and soul and body be preserved blameless unto the coming of our Lord Jesus Christ" (I Thess. 5:23).

THE POWER OF GOD

We cannot have a right conception of God unless we think of Him as all-powerful, as well as all-wise. He who cannot do what he will and perform all his pleasure cannot be God. As God hath a will to resolve what He deems good, so has He power to execute His will. "The power of God is that ability and strength whereby He can bring to pass whatsoever He pleases, whatsoever His infinite wisdom may direct, and whatsoever the infinite purity of His will may resolve. . . . As holiness is the beauty of all God's attributes, so power is that which gives life and action to all the perfections of the Divine nature. How vain would be the eternal counsels, if power did not step in to execute them. Without power His mercy would be but feeble pity, His promises an empty sound, His threatenings a mere scare-crow. God's power is like Himself: infinite, eternal, incomprehensible; it can neither be checked, restrained, nor frustrated by the creature" (S. Charnock).

"God hath spoken once; twice have I heard this, that power belongeth unto God" (Psa. 62:11). "God hath spoken once": nothing more is necessary! Heaven and earth shall pass away, but His word abideth forever. "God hath spoken once": how befitting His Divine majesty! We poor mortals may speak often and yet fail to be heard. He speaks but once and the thunder of His power is heard on a thousand hills. "The Lord also thundered in the heavens, and the Highest gave His voice; hailstones and coals of fire. Yea, He sent out His arrows, and scattered them; and He shot out lightnings, and discomfited them. Then the channels of waters were seen and the foundations of the world were discovered at Thy rebuke, O Lord, at the blast of the breath of Thy nostrils" (Psa. 18:13-15).

"God hath spoken once": behold His unchanging authority. "For who in the heaven can be compared unto the Lord? who among the sons of the mighty can be likened unto the Lord?" (Psa. 89:6). "And all the inhabitants of the earth are reputed as nothing: and He doeth according to His will in the army of heaven, and among the inhabitants of the earth: and none can stay His hand, or say unto Him, What doest Thou?" (Dan. 4:35). This was openly displayed when God became incarnate and tabernacled among men. To the leper He said, "I will, be thou clean, and immediately his leprosy was cleansed" (Matt. 8:3). To one who had lain in the grave four days He cried, "Lazarus, come forth," and the dead came forth. The stormy wind and the angry wave were hushed at a single word from Him. A legion of demons could not resist His authoritative command.

"Power belongeth unto God," and to Him alone. Not a creature in the entire universe has an atom of power save what God delegates. But God's power is not acquired, nor does it depend upon any recognition by any other authority. It belongs to Him inherently. "God's power is like Himself, self-existent, self-sustained. The mightiest of men cannot add so much as a shadow of increased power to the Omnipotent One. He sits on no buttressed throne and leans on no assisting arm. His court is not maintained by His courtiers, nor does it borrow its splendor from His creatures. He is Himself the great central source and Originator of all power" (C. H. Spurgeon). Not only does all creation bear witness to the great power of God, but also to His entire independency of all created things. Listen to His own challenge: "Where wast thou when I laid the foundations of the earth? declare, if thou hast understanding. Who hath laid the measures thereof, if thou knowest? or who hath stretched the line upon it? Whereupon are the foundations thereof fastened or who laid the cornerstone thereof?" (Job 38. 4-6). How completely is the pride of man laid in the dust!

"Power is also used as a name of God, 'the Son of man sitting at the right hand of power' (Mark 14:62), that is, at the right hand of God. God and power are so inseparable that they are reciprocated. As His essence is immense, not to be confined in place; as it is eternal, not to be measured in time; so it is almighty, not to be limited in regard of action" (S. Charnock). "Lo, these are parts of His ways: but how little a portion is heard of Him? but the thunder of His power who can understand?" (Job 26:14). Who is able to count all the monuments of His power? Even that which is displayed of His might in the visible creation is utterly beyond our powers of comprehension, still less are we able to conceive of omnipotence itself. There is infinitely more power lodged in the nature of God than is expressed in all His works.

"Parts of His ways" we behold in creation, providence, redemption, but only a "little part" of His might is seen in them. Remarkably is this brought out in Hab.3:4: "and there was the hiding of His power." It is scarcely possible to imagine anything more grandiloquent than the imagery of this whole chapter, yet nothing in it surpasses the nobility of this statement. The prophet (in vision) beheld the mighty God scattering the hills and overturning the mountains, which one would think afforded an amazing demonstration of His power. Nay, says our verse, that is rather the "hiding" than the displaying of His power. What is meant? This: so inconceivable, so immense, so uncontrollable is the power of Deity, that the fearful convulsions which He works in nature conceal more than they reveal of His infinite might!

It is very beautiful to link together the following passages: "He walketh upon the waves of the sea" (Job 9:8), which expresses God's uncontrollable power. "He walketh in the circuit of Heaven" (Job 22:14), which tells of the immensity of His presence. "He walketh upon the wings of the wind" (Psa. 104:3), which signifies the amazing swiftness of His operations. This last expression is very remarkable. It is not that "He flieth," or "runneth," but that He "walketh" and that, on the very "wings of the wind"—on the most impetuous of the elements, tossed into utmost rage, and sweeping along with almost inconceivable rapidity, yet they are under His feet, beneath His perfect control!

Let us now consider God's power in creation. "The heavens are Thine, the earth also is Thine, as for the world and the fulness thereof, Thou hast founded them. The north and the south Thou hast created them" (Psa. 89:11,12). Before man can work he must have both tools and materials, but God began with nothing, and by His word alone out of nothing made all things. The intellect cannot grasp it. God "spake and it was done, He commanded and it stood fast" (Psa. 33:9). Primeval matter heard His voice. "God said, Let there be ... and it was so" (Gen. 1). Well may we exclaim, "Thou hast a mighty arm: strong is Thy hand, high is Thy right hand" (Psa. 89:13).

"Who, that looks upward to the midnight sky; and, with an eye of reason, beholds its rolling wonders; who can forbear enquiring, Of what were their mighty orbs formed? Amazing to relate, they were produced without materials. They sprung from emptiness itself. The stately fabric of universal nature emerged out of nothing. What instruments were used by the Supreme Architect to fashion the parts with such exquisite niceness, and give so beautiful a polish to the whole? How was it all connected into one finely-proportioned and nobly finished structure? A bare fiat accomplished all. Let them be, said God. He added no more; and at once the marvelous edifice arose, adorned with every beauty, displaying innumerable perfections, and declaring amidst enraptured seraphs its great Creator's praise. 'By the word of the Lord were the heavens made, and all the host of them by the breath of His mouth,' Psa. 150:1" (James Hervey, 1789).

Consider God's power in preservation. No creature has power to preserve itself. "Can the rush grow up without mire? can the flag grow up without water?" (Job 8:11). Both man and beast would perish if there were not herbs for food, and herbs would wither and die if the earth were not refreshed with fruitful showers. Therefore is God called the Preserver of "man and beast" (Psa. 36:6). He "upholdeth all things by the word of His power" (Heb. 1:3). What a marvel of Divine power is the pre-natal life of every human being! That an infant can live at all, and for so many months, in such cramped and filthy quarters, and that without breathing, is unaccountable without the power of God. Truly He "holdeth our soul in life" (Psa. 66:9).

The preservation of the earth from the violence of the sea is another plain instance of God's might. How is that raging element kept pent within those limits wherein He

54

first lodged it, continuing its channel, without overflowing the earth and dashing in pieces the lower part of the creation? The natural situation of the water is to be above the earth, because it is lighter, and to be immediately under the air, because it is heavier. Who restrains the natural quality of it? Certainly man does not, and cannot. It is the fiat of its Creator which alone bridles it: "And said, Hitherto shalt thou come, but no further: and here shall thy proud waves be stayed" (Job 38:11). What a standing monument of the power of God is the preservation of the world!

Consider God's power in government. Take His restraining the malice of Satan. "The devil, as a roaring lion, walketh about, seeking whom he may devour" (I Peter 5:8). He is filled with hatred against God, and with fiendish enmity against men, particularly the saints. He that envied Adam in paradise, envies us the pleasure of enjoying any of God's blessings. Could he have his will, he would treat all the same way he treated Job: he would send fire from heaven on the fruits of the earth, destroying the cattle, cause a wind to overthrow our houses, and cover our bodies with boils. But, little as men may realize it, God bridles him to a large extent, prevents him from carrying out his evil designs, and confines him within His ordinations.

So too God restrains the natural corruption of men. He suffers sufficient outbreakings of sin to show what fearful havoc has been wrought by man's apostasy from his Maker, but who can conceive the frightful lengths to which men would go were God to remove His curbing hand? "Their mouth is full of cursing and bitterness, their feet are swift to shed blood" (Rom. 3). This is the nature of every descendant of Adam. Then what unbridled licentiousness and headstrong folly would triumph in the world, if the power of God did not interpose to lock down the flood-gates of it! See Psa. 93:3,4.

Consider God's power in judgment. When He smites, none can resist Him: see Ezek. 22:14. How terribly this was exemplified at the Flood! God opened the windows of heaven and broke up the great fountains of the deep, and (excepting those in the ark) the entire human race, helpless before the storm of His wrath, was swept away. A shower of fire and brimstone from heaven, and the cities of the plain were exterminated. Pharaoh and all his hosts were impotent when God blew upon them at the Red Sea. What a terrific word is that in Rom. 9:22: "What if God, willing to show wrath, and to make His power known, endured with much long-suffering the vessels of wrath fitted to destruction." God is going to display His mighty power upon the reprobate not merely by incarcerating them in Gehenna, but by supernaturally preserving their bodies as well as souls amid the eternal burnings of the Lake of Fire.

Well may all tremble before such a God! To treat with disrespect One who can crush us more easily than we can a moth, is a suicidal policy. To openly defy Him who is clothed with omnipotence, who can rend us in pieces or cast into Hell any moment He pleases, is the very height of insanity. To put it on its lowest ground, it is but the part of wisdom to heed His command, "Kiss the Son, lest He be angry, and ye perish from the way, when His wrath is kindled but a little" (Psa. 2:12).

Well may the enlightened soul adore such a God! The wondrous and infinite perfections of such a Being call for fervent worship. If men of might and renown claim the admiration of the world, how much more should the power of the Almighty fill us with wonderment and homage. "Who is like unto Thee, O Lord, among the gods, who is like Thee, glorious in holiness, fearful in praises, doing wonders" (Ex. 15:11).

Well may the saint trust such a God! He is worthy of implicit confidence. Nothing is too hard for Him. If God were stinted in might and had a limit to His strength we might well despair. But seeing that He is clothed with omnipotence, no prayer is too hard for Him to answer, no need too great for Him to supply, no passion too strong for Him to subdue; no temptation too powerful for Him to deliver from, no misery too deep for Him to relieve. "The Lord is the strength of my life; of whom shall I be afraid?" (Psa. 27:1). "Now unto Him that is able to do exceeding abundantly above all that we ask or think, according to the power that worketh in us, unto Him be glory in the church by Christ Jesus throughout all ages, world without end. Amen" (Eph. 3:20,21).

THE FAITHFULNESS OF GOD

Unfaithfulness is one of the most outstanding sins of these evil days. In the business world, a man's word is, with exceedingly rare exceptions, no longer his bond. In the social world, marital infidelity abounds on every hand, the sacred bonds of wedlock being broken with as little regard as the discarding of an old garment. In the ecclesiastical realm, thousands who have solemnly covenanted to preach the truth make no scruple to attack and deny it. Nor can reader or writer claim complete immunity from this fearful sin: in how many ways have we been unfaithful to Christ, and to the light and privileges which God has entrusted to us! How refreshing, then, how unspeakably blessed, to lift our eyes above this scene of ruin, and behold One who is faithful, faithful in all things, faithful at all times.

"Know therefore that the Lord thy God, He is God, the faithful God" (Deut. 7:9). This quality is essential to His being, without it He would not be God. For God to be unfaithful would be to act contrary to His nature, which were impossible: "If we believe not, yet He abideth faithful; He cannot deny Himself" (II Tim. 2:13). Faithfulness is one of the glorious perfections of His being. He is as it were clothed with it: "O Lord God of hosts, who is a strong Lord like unto Thee? or to Thy faithfulness round about Thee?" (Psa. 89:8). So too when God became incarnate it was said, "Righteousness shall be the girdle of His loins, and faithfulness the girdle of His reins" (Isa. 11:5).

What a word is that in Psa. 36:5, "Thy mercy, O Lord, is in the heavens; and Thy faithfulness unto the clouds." Far above all finite comprehension is the unchanging faithfulness of God. Everything about God is great, vast, incomparable. He never forgets, never fails, never falters, never forfeits His word. To every declaration of promise or prophecy the Lord has exactly adhered, every engagement of covenant or threatening He will make good, for "God is not a man, that He should lie; neither the son of man, that He should repent: hath He said, and shall He not do it? or hath He spoken, and shall He not make it good?" (Num. 23:19). Therefore does the believer exclaim, "His compassions fail not, they are new every morning: great is Thy faithfulness" (Lam. 3:22,23).

Scripture abounds in illustrations of God's faithfulness. More than four thousand years ago He said, "While the earth remaineth, seedtime and harvest, and cold and heat, and summer and winter, and day and night shall not cease" (Gen. 8:22). Every year that comes furnishes a fresh witness to God's fulfillment of this promise. In Gen. 15 we find that Jehovah declared unto Abraham, "thy seed shall be a stranger in a land that is not theirs, and shall serve them . . . But in the fourth generation they shall come hither again" (vv. 13-16). Centuries ran their weary course. Abraham's descendants groaned amid the brick-kilns of Egypt. Had God forgotten His promise? No, indeed. Read Ex. 12:41, "And it came to pass at the end of the four hundred and thirty years, even the selfsame day it came to pass, that all the hosts of the Lord went out from the land of Egypt." Through Isaiah the Lord declared, "Behold, a virgin shall conceive, and bear a son, and shall call His name Immanuel" (7:14). Again centuries passed, but "When the fulness of the time was come, God sent forth His Son, made of a woman" (Gal. 4:4).

God is true. His Word of Promise is sure. In all His relations with His people God is faithful. He may be safely relied upon. No one ever yet really trusted Him in vain. We find this precious truth expressed almost everywhere in the Scriptures, for His people need to know that faithfulness is an essential part of the Divine character. This is the basis of our confidence in Him. But it is one thing to accept the faithfulness of God as a Divine truth, it is quite another to act upon it. God has given us many "exceeding great and precious promises," but are we really counting on His fulfillment of them? Are we actually expecting Him to do for us all that He has said? Are we resting with implicit assurance on these words, "He is faithful that promised" (Heb. 10:23).

There are seasons in the lives of all when it is not easy, no not even for Christians, to believe that God is faithful. Our faith is sorely tried, our eyes bedimmed with tears, and we can no longer trace the outworkings of His love. Our ears are distracted with the noises of the world, harassed by the atheistic whisperings of Satan, and we can no longer hear the sweet accents of His still small voice. Cherished plans have been thwarted, friends on whom we relied have failed us, a professed brother or sister in Christ has betrayed us. We are staggered. We sought to be faithful to God, and now a dark cloud hides Him from us. We find it difficult, yea, impossible, for carnal reason to harmonize His frowning providence with His gracious promises. Ah, faltering soul, severely-tried fellow-pilgrim, seek grace to heed Isa. 50:10, "Who is among you that feareth the Lord, that obeyeth the voice of His servant, that walketh in darkness and hath no light? let him trust in the name of the Lord, and stay upon his God."

When you are tempted to doubt the faithfulness of God, cry out, "Get thee hence, Satan." Though you cannot now harmonize God's mysterious dealings with the avowals of His love, wait on Him for more light. In His own good time He will make it plain to you. "What I do thou knowest not now, but thou shalt know hereafter" (John 13:7). The sequel will yet demonstrate that God has neither forsaken nor deceived His child. "And therefore will the Lord wait that He may be gracious unto you, and therefore will He be exalted, that He may have mercy upon you: for the Lord is a God of judgment: blessed are all they that wait for Him" (Isa. 30:18).

> "Judge not the Lord by feeble sense,
>   But trust Him for His grace,
> Behind a frowning providence
>   He hides a smiling face.
> Ye fearful saints, fresh courage take,
>   The clouds ye so much dread,
> Are rich with mercy, and shall break
>   In blessing o'er your head."

"Thy testimonies which Thou hast commanded are righteous and very faithful" (Psa. 119:138). God has not only told us the best, but He has not withheld the worst. He has faithfully described the ruin which the Fall has effected. He has faithfully diagnosed the terrible state which sin has produced. He has faithfully made known His inveterate hatred of evil, and that He must punish the same. He has faithfully warned us that He is "a consuming fire" (Heb. 12:29). Not only does His Word abound in illustrations of His fidelity in fulfilling His promises, but it also records numerous examples of His faithfulness in making good His threatenings. Every stage of Israel's history exemplifies that solemn fact. So it was with individuals: Pharaoh, Korah, Achan and a host of others are so many proofs. And thus it will be with you, my reader: unless you have fled or do flee to Christ for refuge, the everlasting burning of the Lake of Fire will be your sure and certain portion. God is faithful.

God is faithful in preserving His people. "God is faithful, by whom ye are called unto the fellowship of His Son" (I Cor. 1:9). In the previous verse promise was made that God would confirm unto the end His own people. The apostle's confidence in the absolute security of believers was founded not on the strength of their resolutions or ability to persevere, but on the veracity of Him that cannot lie. Since God has promised to His Son a certain people for His inheritance, to deliver them from sin and condemnation, and to become the participants of eternal life in glory, it is certain that He will not allow any of them to perish.

God is faithful in disciplining His people. He is faithful in what He withholds, no less than in what He gives. He is faithful in sending sorrow as well as in giving joy. The faithfulness of God is a truth to be confessed by us not only when we are at ease, but also when we are smarting under the sharpest rebuke. Nor must this confession be merely of our mouths, but of our hearts too. When God smites us with the rod of chastisement, it is faithfulness which wields it. To acknowledge this means that we humble ourselves before Him, own that we fully deserve His correction, and instead of murmuring, thank Him for it. God never afflicts without a reason: "For this cause many are weak and sickly among you" (I Cor. 11:30), illustrates this principle. When His rod falls on us let us say with Daniel, "O Lord, righteousness belongeth unto Thee, but unto us confusion of faces" (9:7).

"I know, O Lord, that Thy judgments are right, and that Thou in faithfulness hast afflicted me" (Psa. 119:75). Trouble and affliction are not only consistent with God's love plighted in the everlasting covenant, but they are parts of the administration of the same. God is not only faithful notwithstanding afflictions, but faithful in sending them. "Then will I visit their transgression with the rod, and their iniquity with stripes: My loving kindness will I not utterly take from him nor suffer My faithfulness to fail" (Psa. 89:32,33). Chastening is not only reconcilable with God's loving-kindness, but it is the effect and expression of it. It would much quieten the minds of God's people if they would remember that His covenant love binds Him to lay on them seasonable correction. Afflictions are necessary for us: "In their affliction they will seek Me early" (Hos. 5:15).

God is faithful in glorifying His people. "Faithful is He which calleth you, who also will do" (I Thess. 5:24). The immediate reference here is to the saints being "preserved blameless unto the coming of our Lord Jesus Christ." God treats with us not on the ground of our merits (for we have none), but for His own great name's sake. God is constant to Himself and to His own purpose of grace "whom He called . . . them He also glorified" (Rom. 8:30). God gives a full demonstration of the constancy of His everlasting goodness toward His elect by effectually calling them out of darkness into His marvelous light, and this should fully assure them of the certain continuance of it. "The foundation of God standeth sure" (II Tim. 2:19). Paul was resting on the faithfulness of God when he said,

"I know whom I have believed, and am persuaded that He is able to keep that which I have committed unto Him against that day" (II Tim. 1:12).

The apprehension of this blessed truth will preserve us from worry. To be full of care, to view our situation with dark forebodings, to anticipate the morrow with sad anxiety, is to reflect upon the faithfulness of God. He who has cared for His child through all the years, will not forsake him in old age. He who has heard your prayers in the past, will not refuse to supply your need in the present emergency. Rest on Job 5:19, "He shall deliver thee in six troubles: yea, in seven there shall be no evil touch thee."

The apprehension of this blessed truth will check our murmurings. The Lord knows what is best for each one of us, and one effect of resting on this truth will be the silencing of our petulant complainings. God is greatly honoured when, under trial and chastening, we have good thoughts of Him, vindicate His wisdom and justice, and recognize His love in His very rebukes.

The apprehension of this blessed truth will beget increasing confidence in God. "Wherefore let them that suffer according to the will of God commit the keeping of their souls to Him in well doing, as unto a faithful Creator" (I Peter 4:19). When we trustfully resign ourselves, and all our affairs into God's hands, fully persuaded of His love and faithfulness, the sooner shall we be satisfied with His providences and realize that "He doeth all things well."

THE GOODNESS OF GOD

"The goodness of God endureth continually" (Psa. 52:1). The "goodness" of God respects the perfection of His nature: "God is light, and in Him is no darkness at all" (I John 1:5). There is such an absolute perfection in God's nature and being that nothing is wanting to it or defective in it, and nothing can be added to it to make it better. "He is originally good, good of Himself, which nothing else is; for all creatures are good only by participation and communication from God. He is essentially good; not only good, but goodness itself: the creature's good is a superadded quality, in God it is His essence. He is infinitely good; the creature's good is but a drop, but in God there is an infinite ocean or gathering together of good. He is eternally and immutably good, for He cannot be less good than He is; as there can be no addition made to Him, so no subtraction from Him" (Thos. Manton). God is *summum bonum,* the chiefest good.

The original Saxon meaning of our English word "God" is "The Good." God is not only the Greatest of all beings, but the Best. All the goodness there is in any creature has been imparted from the Creator, but God's goodness is underived, for it is the essence of His eternal nature. As God is infinite in power from all eternity, before there was any display thereof, or any act of omnipotency put forth; so He was eternally good before there was any communication of His bounty, or any creature to

65

whom it might be imparted or exercised. Thus, the first manifestation of this Divine perfection was in giving being to all things. "Thou art good, and doest good" (Psa. 119: 68). God has in Himself an infinite and inexhaustible treasure of all blessedness enough to fill all things.

All that emanates from God—His decrees, His creation, His laws, His providences—cannot be otherwise than good: as it is written. "And God saw everything that He had made, and, behold, it was very good" (Gen. 1:31). Thus, the "goodness" of God is seen, first, in creation. The more closely the creature is studied, the more the beneficence of its Creator becomes apparent. Take the highest of God's earthly creatures, man. Abundant reason has he to say with the Psalmist, "I will praise Thee, for I am fearfully and wonderfully made: marvelous are Thy works, and that my soul knoweth right well" (139:14). Everything about the structure of our bodies attests the goodness of their Maker. How suited the hands to perform their allotted work! How good of the Lord to appoint sleep to refresh the wearied body! How benevolent His provision to give unto the eyes lids and brows for their protection! And so we might continue indefinitely.

Nor is the goodness of the Creator confined to man, it is exercised toward all His creatures. — "The eyes of all wait upon Thee; and Thou givest them their meat in due season. Thou openest Thine hand, and satisfiest the desire of every living thing" (Psa. 145:15,16). Whole volumes might be written, yea have been, to amplify this fact. Whether it be the birds of the air, the beasts of the forest, or the fish in the sea, abundant provision has been made to supply their every need. God "giveth food to all flesh, for His mercy endureth forever" (Psa. 136:25). Truly, "The earth is full of the goodness of the Lord" (Psa. 33:5).

66

The goodness of God is seen in the variety of natural pleasures which He has provided for His creatures. God might have been pleased to satisfy your hunger without the food being pleasing to our palates—how His benevolence appears in the varied flavours which He has given to meats, vegetables, and fruits! God has not only given us senses, but also that which gratifies them; and this too reveals His goodness. The earth might have been as fertile as it is without its being so delightfully variegated. Our physical lives could have been sustained without beautiful flowers to regale our eyes, and exhale sweet perfumes. We might have walked the fields without our ears being saluted by the music of the birds. Whence then, this loveliness, this charm, so freely diffused over the face of nature? Verily, "The tender mercies of the Lord are over all His works" (Psa. 145:9).

The goodness of God is seen in that when man transgressed the law of His Creator a dispensation of unmixed wrath did not at once commence. Well might God have deprived His fallen creatures of every blessing, every comfort, every pleasure. Instead, He ushered in a regime of a mixed nature, of mercy and judgment. This is very wonderful if it be duly considered, and the more thoroughly that regime be examined the more will it appear that "mercy rejoiceth against judgment" (James 2:13). Notwithstanding all the evils which attend our fallen state, the balance of good greatly preponderates. With comparatively rare exceptions, men and women experience a far greater number of days of health, than they do of sickness and pain. There is much more creature-happiness than creature-misery in the world. Even our sorrows admit of considerable alleviation, and God has given to the human mind a pliability which adapts itself to circumstances and makes the most of them.

Nor can the benevolence of God be justly called into question because there is suffering and sorrow in the world. If man sins against the goodness of God, if he despises "the riches of His goodness and forbearance and long-suffering," and after the hardness and impenitency of his heart treasurest up unto himself wrath against the day of wrath (Rom. 2:5,6), who is to blame but himself? Would God be "good" if He punished not those who ill-use His blessings, abuse His benevolence, and trample His mercies beneath their feet? It will be no reflection upon God's goodness, but rather the brightest exemplification of it, when He shall rid the earth of those who have broken His laws, defied His authority, mocked His messengers, scorned His Son, and persecuted those for whom He died.

The goodness of God appeared most illustriously when He sent forth His Son "made of a woman, made under the law, to redeem them that were under the law, that we might receive the adoption of sons" (Gal. 4:4,5). Then it was that a multitude of the heavenly host praised their Maker and said, "Glory to God in the highest and on earth peace, good-will toward men" (Luke 2:14). Yes, in the Gospel the "grace (Gr. benevolence or goodness) of God that bringeth salvation hath appeared to all men" (Titus 2:11). Nor can God's benignity be called into question because He has not made every sinful creature to be a subject of His redemptive grace. He did not the fallen angels. Had God left all to perish it had been no reflection on His goodness. To any who would challenge this statement we will remind him of our Lord's sovereign prerogative: "Is it not lawful for Me to do what I will with Mine own? Is thine eye evil, because I am good?" (Matt. 20:15).

"O that men would praise the Lord for His goodness, and for His wonderful works to the children of men" (Psa. 107:8). Gratitude is the return justly required from the objects of His beneficence; yet is it often withheld from our great Benefactor simply because His goodness is so constant and so abundant. It is lightly esteemed because it is exercised toward us in the common course of events. It is not felt because we daily experience it. "Despisest thou the riches of His goodness?" (Rom. 2:4). His goodness is "despised" when it is not improved as a means to lead men to repentance, but, on the contrary, serves to harden them from the supposition that God entirely overlooks their sin.

The goodness of God is the life of the believer's trust. It is this excellency in God which most appeals to our hearts. Because His goodness endureth forever, we ought never to be discouraged: "The Lord is good, a stronghold in the day of trouble, and He knoweth them that trust in Him" (Nahum 1:7). "When others behave badly to us, it should only stir us up the more heartily to give thanks unto the Lord, because He is good; and when we ourselves are conscious that we are far from being good, we should only the more reverently bless Him that He is good. We must never tolerate an instant's unbelief as to the goodness of the Lord; whatever else may be questioned, this is absolutely certain, that Jehovah is good; His dispensations may vary, but His nature is always the same." (C. H. Spurgeon).

THE PATIENCE OF GOD

Far less has been written upon this than the other excellencies of the Divine character. Not a few of those who have expatiated at length upon the Divine attributes have passed over the patience of God without any comment. It is not easy to suggest a reason for this, for surely the longsuffering of God is as much one of the Divine perfections as is His wisdom, power, or holiness, and as much to be admired and revered by us. True, the actual term will not be found in a concordance so frequently as the others, but the glory of this grace itself shines forth on almost every page of Scripture. Certain it is that we lose much if we do not frequently meditate upon the patience of God and earnestly pray that our hearts and ways may be more completely conformed thereto.

Most probably the principal reason why so many writers have failed to give us anything, separately, upon the patience of God was because of the difficulty of distinguishing this attribute from the Divine goodness and mercy, particularly the latter. God's longsuffering is mentioned in conjunction with His grace and mercy again and again, as may be seen by consulting Ex. 34:6, Num. 14:18, Psa. 86:15, etc. That the patience of God is really a display of His mercy, in fact is one way in which it is frequently manifested, cannot be gainsaid; but that they are one and the same excellency, and are not to be separated, we cannot concede. It may not be easy to discriminate between them, nevertheless, Scripture fully warrants us in predicating some things of the one which we cannot of the other.

Stephen Charnock, the Puritan, defines God's patience, in part, thus: "It is a part of the Divine goodness and mercy, yet differs from both. God being the greatest goodness, hath the greatest mildness; mildness is always the companion of true goodness, and the greater the goodness, the greater the mildness. Who so holy as Christ, and who so meek? God's slowness to anger is a branch of His mercy: 'the Lord is full of compassion, slow to anger' (Psa. 145:8). It differs from mercy in the formal consideration of the subject: mercy respects the creature as miserable, patience respects the creature as criminal; mercy pities him in his misery, patience bears with the sin which engendered the misery, and giving birth to more."

Personally we would define the Divine patience as that power of control which God exercises over Himself, causing Him to bear with the wicked and forebear so long in punishing them. In Nahum 1:3 we read, "The Lord is slow to anger and great in power," upon which Mr. Charnock said, "Men that are great in the world are quick in passion, and are not so ready to forgive an injury, or bear with an offender, as one of a meaner rank. It is a want of power over that man's self that makes him do unbecoming things upon a provocation. A prince that can bridle his passions is a king over himself as well as over his subjects. God is slow to anger because great in power. He has no less power over Himself than over His creatures."

It is at the above point, we think, that God's patience is most clearly distinguished from His mercy. Though the creature is benefitted thereby, the patience of God chiefly respects Himself, a restraint placed upon His acts by His will; whereas His mercy terminates wholly upon the creature. The patience of God is that excellency which causes

Him to sustain great injuries without immediately avenging Himself. Thus the Hebrew word for the Divine longsuffering is rendered "slow to anger" in Nehemiah 9:17, Psa. 103:8, etc. Not that there are any passions in the Divine nature, but that God's wisdom and will is pleased to act with that stateliness and sobriety which becometh His exalted majesty.

In support of our definition above let us point out that it was to this excellency in the Divine character that Moses appealed, when Israel sinned so grievously at Kadesh-Barnea, and there provoked Jehovah so sorely. Unto His servant the Lord said, "I will smite them with the pestilence and disinherit them." Then it was that the typical mediator pleaded, "I beseech Thee let the power of my Lord be great according as Thou hast spoken, saying, The Lord is longsuffering," etc. (Num. 14:17). Thus, His "longsuffering," is His power of self-restraint.

Again, in Rom. 9:22 we read, "What if God, willing to show His wrath, and to make His power known, endured with much longsuffering the vessels of wrath fitted to destruction." Were God to immediately break these reprobate vessels into pieces, His power of self-control would not so eminently appear; by bearing with their wickedness and forebearing punishment so long, the power of His patience is gloriously demonstrated. True, the wicked interpret His longsuffering quite differently—"Because sentence against an evil work is not executed speedily, therefore the heart of the sons of men is fully set in them to do evil" (Eccl. 8:11)—but the anointed eye adores what they abuse.

"The God of patience" (Rom. 15:5) is one of the Divine titles. Deity is thus denominated, first, because God is both the Author and Object of the grace of patience in the creature. Second, because this is what He is in Himself: patience is one of His perfections. Third, as a pattern for us: "Put on therefore, as the elect of God, holy and beloved, bowels of mercy, kindness, humbleness of mind, meekness, longsuffering" (Col. 3:12). And again, "Be ye therefore followers (emulators) of God, as dear children" (Eph. 5:2). When tempted to be disgusted at the dullness of another, or to be revenged on one who has wronged you, call to remembrance God's infinite patience and longsuffering with yourself.

The patience of God is manifested in His dealings with sinners. How strikingly was it displayed toward the antideluvians. When mankind was universally degenerate, and all flesh had corrupted his way, God did not destroy them till He had forewarned them. He "waited" (I Peter 3:20), probably no less than one hundred and twenty years (Gen. 6:3), during which time Noah was a "preacher of righteousness" (II Peter 2:5). So, later, when the Gentiles not only worshipped and served the creature more than the Creator, but also committed the vilest abominations contrary to even the dictates of nature (Rom. 1:19-26), and hereby filled up the measure of their iniquity; yet, instead of drawing His sword for the extermination of such rebels, God "suffered all nations to walk in their own ways" and gave them "rain from heaven and fruitful seasons" (Acts 14:16,17).

Marvelously was God's patience exercised and manifested toward Israel. First, He "suffered their manners" for forty years in the wilderness (Acts 13:18). Later, when they had entered Canaan, but followed the evil customs of the nations around them, and turned to idolatry; though God chastened them sorely, He did not utterly destroy them, but in their distress, raised up deliverers for them. When their iniquity was raised to such a height that none but a God of infinite patience could have borne

73

them, He, notwithstanding, spared them many years before He allowed them to be carried down into Babylon. Finally, when their rebellion against Him reached its climax by crucifying His Son, He waited forty years ere He sent the Romans against them, and that, only after they had judged themselves "unworthy of eternal life" (Acts 13:46).

How wondrous is God's patience with the world today. On every side people are sinning with a high hand. The Divine law is trampled under foot and God Himself openly despised. It is truly amazing that He does not instantly strike dead those who so brazenly defy Him. Why does He not suddenly cut off the haughty infidel and blatant blasphemer, as He did Ananias and Sapphira? Why does He not cause the earth to open its mouth and devour the persecutors of his people, so that, like Dathan and Abiran, they shall go down alive into the Pit? And what of apostate Christendom, where every possible form of sin is now tolerated and practiced under cover of the holy name of Christ? Why does not the righteous wrath of Heaven make an end of such abominations? Only one answer is possible: because God bears with "much longsuffering the vessels of wrath fitted to destruction."

And what of the writer and the reader? Let us review our own lives. It is not long since we followed a multitude to do evil, had no concern for God's glory, and lived only to gratify self. How patiently He bore with our vile conduct! And now that grace has snatched us as brands from the burning, giving us a place in God's family, and begotten us unto an eternal inheritance in glory; how miserably we requite Him. How shallow our gratitude, how tardy our obedience, how frequent our backslidings! One reason why God suffers the flesh to remain in the believer is that He may exhibit His "longsuffering to usward" (II Peter

3:9). Since this Divine attribute is manifested only in this world, God takes advantage to display it toward "His own."

May our meditation upon this Divine excellency soften our hearts, make our consciences tender, and may we learn in the school of holy experience the "patience of saints," namely, submission to the Divine will and continuance in well doing. Let us earnestly seek grace to emulate this Divine excellency. "Be ye therefore perfect, even as your Father which is in heaven is perfect" (Matt. 5:48): in the immediate context Christ exhorts us to love our enemies, bless them that curse us, do good to them that hate us. God bears long with the wicked notwithstanding the multitude of their sin, and shall we desire to be revenged because of a single injury?

THE GRACE OF GOD

This is a perfection of the Divine character which is exercised only toward the elect. Neither in the Old Testament nor in the New is the grace of God ever mentioned in connection with mankind generally, still less with the lower orders of His creatures. In this it is distinguished from "mercy," for the mercy of God is "over all His works" (Psa. 145:9). Grace is the alone source from which flows the goodwill, love, and salvation of God unto His chosen people. This attribute of the Divine character was defined by Abraham Booth in his helpful book, "The Reign of Grace"* thus, "It is the eternal and absolute free favour of God, manifested in the vouchsafement of spiritual and eternal blessings to the guilty and the unworthy."

Divine grace is the sovereign and saving favour of God exercised in the bestowment of blessings upon those who have no merit in them and for which no compensation is demanded from them. Nay, more; it is the favour of God shown to those who not only have no positive deserts of their own, but who are thoroughly ill-deserving and hell-deserving. It is completely unmerited and unsought, and is altogether unattracted by anything in or from or by the objects upon which it is bestowed. Grace can neither be bought, earned, nor won by the creature. If it could be, it would cease to be grace. When a thing is said

*Reiner Publications $2.50

76

to be of "grace" we mean that the recipient has no claim upon it, that it was in nowise due him. It comes to him as pure charity, and, at first, unasked and undesired.

The fullest exposition of the amazing grace of God is to be found in the Epistles of the apostle Paul. In his writings "grace" stands in direct opposition to works and worthiness, all works and worthiness, of whatever kind or degree. This is abundantly clear from Rom. 11:6, "And if by grace, then is it no more of works: otherwise grace is no more grace. If it be of works, then is it no more grace, otherwise work is no more work." Grace and works will no more unite than an acid and an alkali. "By grace are ye saved through faith; and that not of yourselves; it is the gift of God: not of works, lest any man should boast" (Eph. 2:8,9). The absolute favour of God can no more consist with human merit than oil and water will fuse into one: see also Rom. 4:4,5.

There are three principal characteristics of Divine grace. First, it is eternal. Grace was planned before it was exercised, purposed before it was imparted: "Who hath saved us, and called us with a holy calling, not according to our works, but according to His own purpose and grace, which was given us in Christ Jesus before the world began" (II Tim. 1:9). Second, it is free, for none did ever purchase it: "Being justified freely by His grace" (Rom. 3:24). Third, it is sovereign, because God exercises it toward and bestows it upon whom He pleases: "Even so might grace reign" (Rom. 5:21). If grace "reigns" then it is on the throne, and the occupant of the throne is sovereign. Hence, "the throne of grace" (Heb. 4:16).

Just because grace is unmerited favour, it must be exercised in a sovereign manner. Therefore does the Lord declare, "I will be gracious to whom I will be gracious"

(Ex. 33:19). Were God to show grace to all of Adam's descendants, men would at once conclude that He was righteously compelled to take them to heaven as a meet compensation for allowing the human race to fall into sin. But the great God is under no obligation to any of His creatures, least of all to those who are rebels against Him.

Eternal life is a gift, therefore it can neither be earned by good works, nor claimed as a right. Seeing that salvation is a "gift," who has any right to tell God on whom He ought to bestow it? It is not that the Giver ever refuses this gift to any who seek it whole-heartedly, and according to the rules which He has prescribed. No; He refuses none who come to Him empty-handed and in the way of His appointing. But if out of a world of impenitent and unbelieving, God is determined to exercise His sovereign right by choosing a limited number to be saved, who is wronged? Is God obliged to force His gift on those who value it not? Is God compelled to save those who are determined to go their own way?

But nothing more riles the natural man and brings to the surface his innate and inveterate enmity against God than to press upon him the eternality, the freeness, and the absolute sovereignty of Divine grace. That God should have formed His purpose from everlasting, without in anywise consulting the creature, is too abasing for the unbroken heart. That grace cannot be earned or won by any efforts of man is too self-emptying for self-righteousness. And that grace singles out whom it pleases to be its favoured objects, arouses hot protests from haughty rebels. The clay rises up against the Potter and asks, "Why hast Thou made me thus?" A lawless insurrectionist dares to call into question the justice of Divine sovereignty.

The distinguishing grace of God is seen in saving that people whom He has sovereignly singled out to be His high favourites. By "distinguishing" we mean that grace discriminates, makes differences, chooses some and passes by others. It was distinguishing grace which selected Abraham from the midst of his idolatrous neighbors and made him "the friend of God." It was distinguishing grace which saved "publicans and sinners," but said of the religious Pharisees, "Let them alone" (Matt. 15:14). Nowhere does the glory of God's free and sovereign grace shine more conspicuously than in the unworthiness and unlikeness of its objects. Beautifully was this illustrated by James Hervey, (1751):

"Where sin has abounded, says the proclamation from the court of heaven, grace doth much more abound. Manasseh was a monster of barbarity, for he caused his own children to pass through the fire, and filled Jerusalem with innocent blood. Manasseh was an adept in iniquity, for he not only multiplied, and to an extravagant degree, his own sacrilegious impieties, but he poisoned the principles and perverted the manners of his subjects, making them do worse than the most detestable of the heathen idolators: see II Chron. 33. Yet, through this superabundant grace he is humbled, he is reformed, and becomes a child of forgiving love, an heir of immortal glory.

"Behold that bitter and bloody persecutor, Saul; when breathing out threatenings and bent upon slaughter, he worried the lambs and put to death the disciples of Jesus. The havoc he had committed, the inoffensive families he had already ruined, were not sufficient to assuage his vengeful spirit. They were only a taste, which, instead of glutting the bloodhound, made him more closely pursue the track, and more eagerly pant for destruction. He is still thirsty for violence and murder. So eager and insatiable is his thirst, that he even breathes out threatening and slaughter (Acts 9:1). His words are spears and arrows, and his tongue a sharp sword. 'Tis as natural for him to menace the Christians as to breathe the air. Nay, they bled every hour in the purposes of his rancorous heart. It is only owing to want of power that every syllable he utters, every breath he draws, does not deal out deaths, and cause some of the innocent disciples to fall. Who, upon the principles of human judgment, would not have pronounced him a vessel of wrath, destined to unavoidable damnation? Nay, who would not have been ready to conclude that, if there were heavier chains and a deeper dungeon in the world of woe, they must surely be reserved for such an implacable enemy of true godliness? Yes, admire and adore the inexhaustible treasures of grace—this Saul is admitted into the goodly fellowship of the prophets, is numbered with the noble army of martyrs and makes a distinguished figure among the glorious company of the apostles.

"The Corinthians were flagitious even to a proverb. Some of them wallowing in such abominable vices, and habituated themselves to such outrageous acts of injustice, as were a reproach to human nature. Yet, even these sons of violence and slaves of sensuality were washed, sanctified, justified (I Cor. 6:9-11). 'Washed,' in the precious blood of a dying Redeemer; 'sanctified,' by the powerful operations of the blessed Spirit; 'justified,' through the infinitely tender mercies of a gracious God. Those who were once the burden of the earth, are now the joy of heaven, the delight of angels."

Now the grace of God is manifested in and by and through the Lord Jesus Christ. "The law was given by Moses, grace and truth came by Jesus Christ" (John 1:17). This does not mean that God never exercised grace toward any before His Son became incarnate—Gen. 6:8, Ex. 33:19, etc., clearly show otherwise. But grace and truth were fully revealed and perfectly exemplified when the Redeemer came to this earth, and died for His people upon the cross. It is through Christ the Mediator alone that the grace of God flows to His elect. "Much more the grace of God, and the gift by grace, which is by one man, Jesus Christ . . . much more they which receive abundance of grace, and of the gift of righteousness, shall reign in life by one, Jesus Christ . . . so might grace reign, through righteousness, unto eternal life, by Jesus Christ our Lord" (Rom. 5:15,17,21).

The grace of God is proclaimed in the Gospel (Acts 20:24), which is to the self-righteous Jew a "stumbling block," and to the conceited and philosophizing Greek "foolishness." And why so? Because there is nothing whatever in it that is adapted to gratify the pride of man. It announces that unless we are saved by grace, we cannot be saved at all. It declares that apart from Christ, the unspeakable Gift of God's grace, the state of every man is desperate, irremediable, hopeless. The Gospel addresses men as guilty, condemned, perishing criminals. It declares that the chastest moralist is in the same terrible plight as is the most voluptuous profligate; that the zealous professor, with all his religious performances, is no better off than the most profane infidel.

The Gospel contemplates every descendant of Adam as a fallen, polluted, hell-deserving and helpless sinner. The grace which the Gospel publishes is his only hope. All stand before God convicted as transgressors of His holy law, as guilty and condemned criminals; awaiting not sentence, but the execution of sentence already passed on them (John 3:18; Rom. 3:19). To complain against the partiality of grace is suicidal. If the sinner insists upon bare justice, then the Lake of Fire must be his eternal portion. His only hope lies in bowing to the sentence which Divine justice has passed upon him, owning the absolute righteousness of it, casting himself on the mercy of God, and stretching forth empty hands to avail himself of the grace of God now made known to him in the Gospel.

The third Person in the Godhead is the Communicator of grace, therefore is He denominated "the spirit of grace" (Zech. 12:10). God the Father is the Fountain of all grace, for He purposed in Himself the everlasting covenant of redemption. God the Son is the only Channel of grace. The Gospel is the Publisher of grace. The Spirit is the Bestower. He is the One who applies the Gospel in saving power to the soul: quickening the elect while spiritually dead, conquering their rebellious wills, melting their hard hearts, opening their blind eyes, cleansing them from the leprosy of sin. Thus we may say with the late G. S. Bishop, "Grace is a provision for men who are so fallen that they cannot lift the axe of justice, so corrupt that they cannot change their own natures, so averse to God that they cannot turn to Him, so blind that they cannot see Him, so deaf that they cannot hear Him, and so dead that He Himself must open their graves and lift them into resurrection."*

*"Grace In Galatians," Reiner Publications, $1.95.

THE MERCY OF GOD

"O Give thanks unto the Lord: for He is good, for His mercy endureth forever" (Psa. 136:1). For this perfection of the Divine character God is greatly to be praised. Three times over in as many verses does the Psalmist here call upon the saints to give thanks unto the Lord for this adorable attribute. And surely this is the least that can be asked for from those who have been such bounteous gainers by it. When we contemplate the characteristics of this Divine excellency, we cannot do otherwise than bless God for it. His mercy is "great" (I Kings 3:6), "plenteous" (Psa. 86:5), "tender" (Luke 1:78), "abundant" (I Peter 1:3); it is "from everlasting to everlasting upon them that fear Him" (Psa. 103:17). Well may we say with the Psalmist, "I will sing aloud of Thy mercy" (Psa. 59:16).

"I will make all My goodness pass before thee, and I will proclaim the name of the Lord before thee; and will be gracious to whom I will be gracious, and will show mercy on whom I will show mercy" (Ex. 33:19). Wherein differs the "mercy" of God from His "grace"? The mercy of God has its spring in the Divine goodness. The first issue of God's goodness is His benignity or bounty, by which He gives liberally to His creatures as creatures; thus has He given being and life to all things. The second issue of God's goodness is His mercy, which denotes the ready inclination of God to relieve the misery of fallen creatures. Thus, "mercy" presupposes sin.

Though it may not be easy at the first consideration to perceive a real difference between the grace and the mercy of God, it helps us thereto if we carefully ponder His dealings with the unfallen angels. He has never exercised mercy toward them, for they have never stood in any need thereof, not having sinned or come beneath the effects of the curse. Yet, they certainly are the objects of God's free and sovereign grace. First, because of His election of them from out of the whole angelic race (I Tim. 5:21). Second, and in consequence of their election, because of His preservation of them from apostasy, when Satan rebelled and dragged down with him one-third of the celestial hosts (Rev. 12:4). Third, in making Christ their Head (Col. 2:10; I Peter 3:22), whereby they are eternally secured in the holy condition in which they were created. Fourth, because of the exalted position which has been assigned them: to live in God's immediate presence (Dan. 7:10), to serve Him constantly in His heavenly temple, to receive honourable commissions from Him (Heb. 1:14). This is abundant grace toward them; but "mercy" it is not.

In endeavoring to study the mercy of God as it is set forth in Scripture, a threefold distinction needs to be made, if the Word of Truth is to be "rightly divided" thereon. First, there is a general mercy of God, which is extended not only to all men, believers and unbelievers alike, but also to the entire creation: "His tender mercies are over all His works" (Psa. 145:9): "He giveth to all life, and breath, and all things" (Acts 17:25). God has pity upon the brute creation in their needs, and supplies them with suitable provision. Second, there is a special

84

mercy of God, which is exercised toward the children of men, helping and succouring them, notwithstanding their sins. To them also He communicates all the necessities of life: "for He maketh His sun to rise on the evil and on the good, and sendeth rain on the just and on the unjust" (Matt. 5:45). Third, there is a sovereign mercy which is reserved for the heirs of salvation, which is communicated to them in a covenant way, through the Mediator.

Following out a little further the difference between the second and third distinctions pointed out above, it is important to note that the mercies which God bestows on the wicked are solely of a temporal nature; that is to say, they are confined strictly to this present life. There will be no mercy extended to them beyond the grave: "It is a people of no understanding: therefore He that made them will not have mercy on them, and He that formed them will show them no favour" (Isa. 27:11). But at this point a difficulty may suggest itself to some of our readers, namely, Does not Scripture affirm that "His mercy endureth forever" (Psa. 136:1)? Two things need to be pointed out in that connection. God can never cease to be merciful, for this is a quality of the Divine essence (Psa. 116:5); but the exercise of His mercy is regulated by His sovereign will. This must be so, for there is nothing outside Himself which obliges Him to act; if there were, that "something" would be supreme, and God would cease to be God.

It is pure sovereign grace which alone determines the exercise of Divine mercy. God expressly affirms this fact in Rom. 9:15, "For He saith to Moses, I will have mercy on whom I will have mercy." It is not the wretchedness of the creature which causes Him to show mercy, for God is not influenced by things outside of Himself as we are. If God were influenced by the abject misery of leprous sinners, He would cleanse and save all of them. But He does not. Why? Simply because it is not His pleasure and purpose so to do. Still less is it the merits of the creature which causes Him to bestow mercies upon them, for it is a contradiction in terms to speak of meriting "mercy." "Not by works of righteousness which we have done, but according to His mercy He saved us" (Titus 3:5)—the one standing in direct antithesis from the other. Nor is it the merits of Christ which moves God to bestow mercies on His elect: that would be putting the effect for the cause. It is "through" or because of the tender mercy of our God that Christ was sent here to His people (Luke 1:78). The merits of Christ make it possible for God to righteously bestow spiritual mercies on His elect, justice having been fully satisfied by the Surety! No, mercy arises solely from God's imperial pleasure.

Again; though it be true, blessedly and gloriously true, that God's mercy "endureth forever," yet we must observe carefully the objects to whom His "mercy" is shown. Even the casting of the reprobate into the Lake of Fire is an act of mercy. The punishment of the wicked is to be contemplated from a threefold viewpoint. From God's side, it is an act of justice, vindicating His honour. The mercy of God is never shown to the prejudice of His holiness and righteousness. From their side, it is an act of equity, when they are made to suffer the due reward of their iniquities. But from the standpoint of the redeemed, the punishment of the wicked is an act of unspeakable mercy. How dreadful would it be if the present order of things should continue forever, when the children of God are obliged to live in the midst of the children of the Devil! Heaven would at once cease to be heaven if the ears of the saints still heard the blasphemous and filthy language of the reprobate. What a mercy that in the New Jerusalem "there shall in no wise enter into it any thing that defileth, neither worketh abomination" (Rev. 21:27)!

Lest the reader might think that in the last paragraph we have been drawing upon our imagination, let us appeal to Holy Scripture in support of what has been said. In Psa. 143:12 we find David praying, "And of Thy mercy cut off mine enemies, and destroy all them that afflict my soul: for I am Thy servant." Again; in Psa. 136:15 we read that God "Overthrew Pharaoh and his hosts in the Red Sea: for His mercy endureth forever." It was an act of vengeance upon Pharaoh and his hosts, but it was an act of "mercy" unto the Israelites. Again, in Rev. 19:1-3 we read, "I heard a great voice of much people in heaven, saying Alleluia; Salvation, and glory, and honour, and power, unto the Lord our God: for true and righteous are His judgments: for He hath judged the great whore, which did corrupt the earth with her fornication, and hath avenged the blood of His servants at her hand. And again they said, Alleluia. And her smoke rose up forever and ever."

From what has just been before us, let us note how vain is the presumptuous hope of the wicked, who, notwithstanding their continued defiance of God, nevertheless count upon His being merciful to them. How many there are who say, I do not believe that God will ever cast me into Hell; He is too merciful. Such a hope is a viper, which if cherished in their bosoms will sting them to death. God is a God of justice as well as mercy, and He has expressly declared that He will "by no means clear the guilty" (Ex. 34:7). Yea, He has said, "The wicked shall be turned into hell, all the nations that forget God"

(Psa. 9:17). As well might men reason: I do not believe that if filth be allowed to accumulate and sewerage become stagnant and people deprive themselves of fresh air, that a merciful God will let them fall a prey to a deadly fever. The fact is that those who neglect the laws of health are carried away by disease, notwithstanding God's mercy. Equally true is it that those who neglect the laws of spiritual health shall forever suffer the Second Death.

Unspeakably solemn is it to see so many abusing this Divine perfection. They continue to despise God's authority, trample upon His laws, continue in sin, and yet presume upon His mercy. But God will not be unjust to Himself. God shows mercy to the truly penitent, but not to the impenitent (Luke 13:3). To continue in sin and yet reckon upon Divine mercy remitting punishment is diabolical. It is saying. "Let us do evil that good may come," and of all such it is written, "whose damnation is just" (Rom. 3:8). Presumption shall most certainly be disappointed; read carefully Deut. 29:18-20. Christ is the spiritual mercy-seat, and all who despise and reject His Lordship shall "perish from the way, when His wrath is kindled but a little" (Psa. 2:12).

But let our final thought be of God's spiritual mercies unto His own people. "Thy mercy is great unto the heavens" (Psa. 57:10). The riches thereof transcend our loftiest thought. "For as the heaven is high above the earth, so great is His mercy toward them that fear Him" (Psa. 103:11). None can measure it. The elect are designated "vessels of mercy" (Rom. 9:23). It is mercy that quickened them when they were dead in sins (Eph. 2:4,5). It is mercy that saves them (Titus 3:5). It is His abundant mercy which begat them unto an eternal inheritance (I Peter 1:3). Time would fail us to tell of His preserving, sustaining, pardoning, supplying mercy. Unto His own, God is "the Father of mercies" (II Cor. 1:3).

> "When all Thy mercies, O my God,
>   My rising soul surveys,
> Transported with the view I'm lost,
>   In wonder, love, and praise."

THE LOVE OF GOD

There are three things told us in Scripture concerning the nature of God. First, "God is spirit" (John 4:24). In the Greek there is no indefinite article, and to say "God is a spirit" is most objectionable, for it places Him in a class with others. God is "spirit" in the highest sense. Because He is "spirit" He is incorporeal, having no visible substance. Had God a tangible body, He would not be omnipresent, He would be limited to one place; because He is "spirit" He fills heaven and earth. Second, "God is light" (I John 1:5), which is the opposite of darkness. In Scripture "darkness" stands for sin, evil, death; and "light" for holiness, goodness, life. "God is light" means that He is the sum of all excellency. Third, "God is love" (I John 4:8). It is not simply that God "loves," but that He is Love itself. Love is not merely one of His attributes, but His very nature.

There are many today who talk about the love of God, who are total strangers to the God of love. The Divine love is commonly regarded as a species of amiable weakness, a sort of good-natured indulgence; it is reduced to a mere sickly sentiment, patterned after human emotion. Now the truth is that on this, as on everything else, our thoughts need to be formed and regulated by what is revealed thereon in Holy Scripture. That there is urgent need for this is apparent not only from the ignorance which so generally prevails, but also from the low state of spirituality which is now so sadly evident everywhere among professing Christians. How little real love there is for God. One chief reason for this is because our hearts are so little occupied with His wondrous love for His people. The better we are acquainted with His love—its character, fulness, blessedness—the more will our hearts be drawn out in love to Him.

1. The love of God is uninfluenced. By this we mean, there was nothing whatever in the objects of His love to call it into exercise, nothing in the creature to attract or prompt it. The love which one creature has for another is because of something in them; but the love of God is free, spontaneous, uncaused. The only reason why God loves any is found in His own sovereign will: "The Lord did not set His love upon you, nor choose you because ye were more in number than any people; for ye were the fewest of all people: but because the Lord loved thee" (Deut. 7:7,8). God has loved His people from everlasting, and therefore nothing of the creature can be the cause of what is found in God from eternity. He loves from Himself: "according to His own purpose" (II Tim. 1:9).

"We love Him, because He first loved us" (I John 4:19). God did not love us because we loved Him, but He loved us before we had a particle of love for Him. Had God loved us in return for ours, then it would not be spontaneous on His part; but because He loved us when we were loveless, it is clear that His love was uninfluenced. It is highly important if God is to be honoured and the heart of His child established, that we should be quite clear upon this precious truth. God's love for me, and for each of "His own," was entirely unmoved by anything in them. What was there in me to attract the heart of God? Absolutely nothing. But, to the contrary, everything to repel Him, everything calculated to make Him

91

loathe me—sinful, depraved, a mass of corruption, with "no good thing" in me.

> "What was there in me that could merit esteem,
>   Or give the Creator delight?
> 'Twas even so, Father, I ever must sing,
>   Because it seemed good in Thy sight."

2. It is eternal. This of necessity. God Himself is eternal, and God is love; therefore, as God Himself had no beginning, His love had none. Granted that such a concept far transcends the grasp of our feeble minds, nevertheless, where we cannot comprehend, we can bow in adoring worship. How clear is the testimony of Jer. 31:3, "I have loved thee with an everlasting love, therefore with loving-kindness have I drawn thee." How blessed to know that the great and holy God loved His people before heaven and earth were called into existence, that He had set His heart upon them from all eternity. Clear proof is this that His love is spontaneous, for He loved them endless ages before they had any being.

The same precious truth is set forth in Eph. 1:4,5, "According as He hath chosen us in Him before the foundation of the world, that we should be holy and without blame before Him. In love having predestinated us." What praise should this evoke from each of His children! How tranquilizing for the heart: since God's love toward me had no beginning, it can have no ending! Since it be true that "from everlasting to everlasting" He is God, and since God is "love," then it is equally true that "from everlasting to everlasting" He loves His people.

3. It is sovereign. This also is self-evident. God Himself is sovereign, under obligations to none, a law unto Himself, acting always according to His own imperial pleasure. Since God be sovereign, and since He be love, it necessarily follows that His love is sovereign. Because

God is God, He does as He pleases; because God is love, He loves whom He pleases. Such is His own express affirmation: "Jacob have I loved, but Esau have I hated" (Rom. 9:19). There was no more reason in Jacob why he should be the object of Divine love, than there was in Esau. They both had the same parents, and were born at the same time, being twins: yet God loved the one and hated the other! Why? Because it pleased Him to do so.

The sovereignty of God's love necessarily follows from the fact that it is uninfluenced by anything in the creature. Thus, to affirm that the cause of His love lies in God Himself, is only another way of saying, He loves whom He pleases. For a moment, assume the opposite. Suppose God's love were regulated by anything else than His will, in such a case He would love by rule, and loving by rule He would be under a law of love, and then so far from being free, God would Himself be ruled by law. "In love having predestinated us unto the adoption of children by Jesus Christ to Himself, according to"—what? Some excellency which He foresaw in them? No; what then: "according to the good pleasure of His will" (Eph. 1:4,5).

4. It is infinite. Everything about God is infinite. His essence fills heaven and earth. His wisdom is illimitable, for He knows everything of the past, present and future. His power is unbounded, for there is nothing too hard for Him. So His love is without limit. There is a depth to it which none can fathom; there is a height to it which none can scale; there is a length and breadth to it which defies measurement, by any creature-standard. Beautifully is this intimated in Eph. 2:4 "But God, who is rich in mercy, for His great love wherewith He loved us": the word "great" there is parallel with the "God so loved" of John 3:16. It tells us that the love of God is so transcendent it cannot be estimated.

"No tongue can fully express the infinitude of God's love, or any mind comprehend it: it 'passeth knowledge' (Eph. 3:19). The most extensive ideas that a finite mind can frame about Divine love, are infinitely below its true nature. The heaven is not so far above the earth as the goodness of God is beyond the most raised conceptions which we are able to form of it. It is an ocean which swells higher than all the mountains of opposition in such as are the objects of it. It is a fountain from which flows all necessary good to all those who are interested in it" (John Brine, 1743).

5. It is immutable. As with God Himself there is "no variableness, neither shadow of turning" (James 1:17), so His love knows neither change or diminution. The worm Jacob supplies a forceful example of this: "Jacob have I loved," declared Jehovah, and despite all his unbelief and waywardness, He never ceased to love him. John 13:1 furnishes another beautiful illustration. That very night one of the apostles would say, "Show us the Father"; another would deny Him with cursings; all of them would be scandalized by and forsake Him. Nevertheless, "having loved His own which were in the world, He loved them unto the end." The Divine love is subject to no vicissitudes. Divine love is "strong as death . . . many waters cannot quench it" (Song of Sol. 8:6,7). Nothing can separate from it: Rom. 8:35-39.

> "His love no end nor measure knows,
>   No change can turn its course,
> Eternally the same it flows
>   From one eternal source."

6. It is holy. God's love is not regulated by caprice, passion, or sentiment, but by principle. Just as His grace reigns not at the expense of it, but "through righteousness" (Rom. 5:21), so His love never conflicts with His

holiness. "God is light" (I John 1:5) is mentioned before "God is love" (I John 4:8). God's love is no mere amiable weakness, or effeminate softness. Scripture declares, "whom the Lord loveth He chasteneth, and scourgeth every son whom He receiveth" (Heb. 12:6). God will not wink at sin, even in His own people. His love is pure, unmixed with any maudlin sentimentality.

7. It is gracious. The love and favour of God are inseparable. This is clearly brought out in Rom. 8:32-39. What that love is from which there can be no "separation," is easily perceived from the design and scope of the immediate context: it is that goodwill and grace of God which determined Him to give His Son for sinners. That love was the impulsive power of Christ's incarnation: "God so loved the world that He gave His only begotten Son" (John 3:16. Christ died not in order to make God love us, but because He did love His people. Calvary is the supreme demonstration of Divine love. Whenever you are tempted to doubt the love of God, Christian reader, go back to Calvary.

Here then is abundant cause for trust and patience under Divine affliction. Christ was beloved of the Father, yet He was not exempted from poverty, disgrace, and persecution. He hungered and thirsted. Thus, it was not incompatible with God's love for Christ when He permitted men to spit upon and smite Him. Then let no Christian call into question God's love when he is brought under painful afflictions and trials. God did not enrich Christ on earth with temporal prosperity, for "He had not where to lay His head." But He did give Him the Spirit "without measure" (John 3:34). Learn then that spiritual blessings are the principal gifts of Divine love. How blessed to know that when the world hates us, God loves us!

THE WRATH OF GOD

It is sad to find so many professing Christians who appear to regard the wrath of God as something for which they need to make an apology, or at least they wish there were no such thing. While some would not go so far as to openly admit that they consider it a blemish on the Divine character, yet they are far from regarding it with delight, they like not to think about it, and they rarely hear it mentioned without a secret resentment rising up in their hearts against it. Even with those who are more sober in their judgment, not a few seem to imagine that there is a severity about the Divine wrath which is too terrifying to form a theme for profitable contemplation. Others harbour the delusion that God's wrath is not consistent with His goodness, and so seek to banish it from their thoughts.

Yes, many there are who turn away from a vision of God's wrath as though they were called to look upon some blotch in the Divine character, or some blot upon the Divine government. But what saith the Scriptures? As we turn to them we find that God has made no attempt to conceal the fact of His wrath. He is not ashamed to make it known that vengeance and fury belong unto Him. His own challenge is, "See now that I, even I, am He, and there is no god with Me: I kill, and I make alive; I wound, and I heal; neither is there any that can deliver out of My hand. For I lift up My hand to heaven, and say, I live forever. If I whet My glittering sword, and Mine hand take hold on judgment; I will render vengeance to Mine enemies, and will reward them that hate Me" (Deut. 32: 39-41). A study of the concordance will show that there are more references in Scripture to the anger, fury, and wrath of God, than there are to His love and tenderness. Because God is holy, He hates all sin; and because He hates all sin, His anger burns against the sinner: Psa. 7:11.

Now the wrath of God is as much a Divine perfection as is His faithfulness, power, or mercy. It must be so, for there is no blemish whatever, not the slightest defect in the character of God; yet there would be if "wrath" were absent from Him! Indifference to sin is a moral blemish, and he who hates it not is a moral leper. How could He who is the Sum of all excellency look with equal satisfaction upon virtue and vice, wisdom and folly? How could He who is infinitely holy disregard sin and refuse to manifest His "severity" (Rom. 9:12) toward it? How could He who delights only in that which is pure and lovely, not loathe and hate that which is impure and vile? The very nature of God makes Hell as real a necessity, as imperatively and eternally requisite, as Heaven is. Not only is there no imperfection in God, but there is no perfection in Him that is less perfect than another.

The wrath of God is eternal detestation of all unrighteousness. It is the displeasure and indignation of Divine equity against evil. It is the holiness of God stirred into activity against sin. It is the moving cause of that just sentence which He passes upon evil-doers. God is angry against sin because it is a rebelling against His authority, a wrong done to His inviolable sovereignty. Insurrectionists against God's government shall be made to know that God is the Lord. They shall be made to feel how great that Majesty is which they despise, and how dreadful is that

97

threatened wrath which they so little regarded. Not that God's anger is a malignant and malicious retaliation, inflicting injury for the sake of it, or in return for injury received. No; while God will vindicate His dominion as the Governor of the universe, He will not be vindictive.

That Divine wrath is one of the perfections of God is not only evident from the considerations presented above, but is also clearly established by the express declarations of His own Word. "For the wrath of God is revealed from heaven" (Rom. 1:18). "It was revealed when the sentence of death was first pronounced, the earth cursed, and man driven out of the earthly paradise; and afterwards by such examples of punishment as those of the Deluge and the destruction of the Cities of the Plain by fire from heaven; but especially by the reign of death throughout the world. It was proclaimed in the curse of the law on every transgression, and was intimated in the institution of sacrifice. In the 8th of Romans, the apostle calls the attention of believers to the fact that the whole creation has become subject to vanity, and groaneth and travaileth together in pain. The same creation which declares that there is a God, and publishes His glory, also proclaims that He is the Enemy of sin and the Avenger of the crimes of men. But above all, the wrath of God was revealed from heaven when the Son of God came down to manifest the Divine character, and when that wrath was displayed in His sufferings and death, in a manner more awful than by all the tokens God had before given of His displeasure against sin. Besides this, the future and eternal punishment of the wicked is now declared in terms more solemn and explicit than formerly. Under the new dispensation there are two revelations given from heaven, one of wrath, the other of grace" (Robt. Haldane).

Again; that the wrath of God is a Divine perfection

98

is plainly demonstrated by what we read of in Psa. 95:11, "Unto whom I sware in My wrath." There are two occasions of God "swearing": in making promises (Gen. 22:16), and in denouncing threatening (Deut. 1:34). In the former, He swares in mercy to His children; in the latter, He swares to terrify the wicked. An oath is for solemn confirmation: Heb. 6:16. In Gen. 22:16 God said, "By Myself have I sworn." In Psa. 89:35 He declares, "Once have I sworn by My holiness." While in Psa. 95:11 He affirmed, "I swear in My wrath." Thus the great Jehovah Himself appeals to His "wrath" as a perfection equal to His "holiness": He swares by the one as much as by the other! Again; as in Christ "dwelleth all the fulness of the Godhead bodily" (Col. 2:9), and as all the Divine perfections are illustriously displayed by Him (John 1:18), therefore do we read of "the wrath of the Lamb" (Rev. 6:16).

The wrath of God is a perfection of the Divine character upon which we need to frequently meditate. First, that our hearts may be duly impressed by God's detestation of sin. We are ever prone to regard sin lightly, to gloss over its hideousness, to make excuses for it. But the more we study and ponder God's abhorrence of sin and His frightful vengeance upon it, the more likely are we to realize its heinousness. Second, to beget a true fear in our souls for God: "Let us have grace whereby we may serve God acceptably with reverence and godly fear: for our God is a consuming fire" (Heb. 12:28,29). We cannot serve Him "acceptably" unless there is due "reverence" for His awful Majesty and "godly fear" of His righteous anger, and these are best promoted by frequently calling to mind that "our God is a consuming fire." Third, to draw out our souls in fervent praise for having delivered us from "the wrath to come" (I Thess. 1:10).

Our readiness or our reluctancy to meditate upon the wrath of God becomes a sure test of how our hearts really stand affected toward Him. If we do not truly rejoice in God, for what He is in Himself, and that because of all the perfections which are eternally resident in Him, then how dwelleth the love of God in us? Each of us needs to be most prayerfully on his guard against devising an image of God in our thoughts which is patterned after our own evil inclinations. Of old the Lord complained, "Thou thoughtest that I was altogether as thyself" (Psa. 50:21), If we rejoice not "at the remembrance of His holiness" (Psa. 97:12), if we rejoice not to know that in a soon-coming Day God will make a most glorious display of His wrath, by taking vengeance on all who now oppose Him, it is proof positive that our hearts are not in subjection to Him, that we are yet in our sins, on the way to the everlasting burnings.

"Rejoice, O ye nations (Gentiles) His people, for He will avenge the blood of His servants, and will render vengeance to His adversaries" (Deut. 32:43). And again we read, "I heard a great voice of much people in heaven, saying Alleluia; Salvation, and glory, and honour, and power, unto the Lord our God; For true and righteous are His judgments: for He hath judged the great whore, which did corrupt the earth with her fornication, and hath avenged the blood of His servants at her hand. And again they said Alleluia" (Rev. 19:1). Great will be the rejoicing of the saints in that day when the Lord shall vindicate His majesty, exercise His awful dominion, magnify His justice, and overthrow the proud rebels who have dared to defy Him.

"If thou Lord, shouldest mark (impute) iniquities, O Lord, who shall stand?" (Psa. 130:3). Well may each of us ask this question, for it is written "the ungodly shall not stand in the judgment" (Psa. 1:5). How sorely was Christ's soul exercised with thoughts of God's marking the iniquities of His people when they were upon Him! He was "amazed and very heavy" (Mark 14:33). His awful agony, His bloody sweat, His strong cries and supplications (Heb. 5:7), His reiterated prayers "If it be possible, let this cup pass from Me," His last dreadful cry, "My God, My God, why hast Thou forsaken Me?" all manifest what fearful apprehensions He had of what it was for God to "mark iniquities." Well may poor sinners cry out, Lord who shall "stand" when the Son of God Himself so trembled beneath the weight of His wrath? If thou, my reader, hast not "fled for refuge" to Christ, the only Saviour, "how wilt thou do in the swelling of the Jordan" (Jer. 12:5)?

"When I consider how the goodness of God is abused by the greatest part of mankind, I cannot but be of his mind that said, The greatest miracle in the world is God's patience and bounty to an ungrateful world. If a prince hath an enemy got into one of his towns, he doth not send them in provision, but lays close siege to the place, and doth what he can to starve them. But the great God, that could wink all His enemies into destruction, bears with them, and is at daily cost to maintain them. Well may He command us to bless them that curse us, who Himself does good to the evil and unthankful. But think not, sinners, that you shall escape thus; God's mill goes slow, but grinds small; the more admirable His patience and bounty now is, the more dreadful and unsupportable will that fury be which ariseth out of His abused goodness. Nothing smoother than the sea, yet when stirred into a tempest, nothing rageth more. Nothing so sweet as the patience and goodness of God, and nothing so terrible as His wrath when it takes fire" (Wm. Gurnall, 1660). Then "flee," my reader, flee to Christ; "flee from the wrath to come" (Matt.

101

3:7) ere it be too late. Do not, we earnestly beseech you, suppose that this message is intended for somebody else. It is to you! Do not be contented by thinking you have already fled to Christ. Make certain! Beg the Lord to search your heart and show you yourself.

* * * * *

A Word to Preachers. Brethren, do we in our oral ministry, preach on this solemn subject as much as we ought? The Old Testament prophets frequently told their hearers that their wicked lives provoked the Holy One of Israel, and that they were treasuring up to themselves wrath against the day of wrath. And conditions in the world are no better now than they were then! Nothing is so calculated to arouse the careless and cause carnal professors to search their hearts, as to enlarge upon the fact that "God is angry with the wicked every day" (Psa. 7:11). The forerunner of Christ warned his hearers to "Flee from the wrath to come" (Matt. 3:7). The Saviour bade His auditors "Fear Him, which after He hath killed, hath power to cast into Hell; yea, I say unto you, Fear Him" (Luke 12:5). The apostle Paul said, "Knowing therefore the terror of the Lord, we persuade men" (II Cor. 5:11). Faithfulness demands that we speak as plainly about Hell as about Heaven.

102

THE CONTEMPLATION OF GOD

In the previous chapters we have had in review some of the wondrous and lovely perfections of the Divine character. From this most feeble and faulty contemplation of His attributes, it should be evident to us all that God is, first, an incomprehensible Being, and, lost in wonder at His infinite greatness, we are constrained to adopt the words of Zophar, "Canst thou by searching find out God? canst thou find out the Almighty unto perfection? It is high as heaven; what canst thou do? deeper than hell; what canst thou know? The measure thereof is longer than the earth, and broader than the sea" (Job 11:7-9). When we turn our thoughts to God's eternity, His immateriality, His omnipresence, His almightiness, our minds are overwhelmed.

But the incomprehensibility of the Divine nature is not a reason why we should desist from reverent inquiry and prayerful strivings to apprehend what He has so graciously revealed of Himself in His Word. Because we are unable to acquire perfect knowledge, it would be folly to say we will therefore make no efforts to attain to any degree of it. It has been well said that, "Nothing will so enlarge the intellect, nothing so magnify the whole soul of man, as a devout, earnest, continued, investigation of the great subject of the Deity. The most excellent study for expanding the soul is the science of Christ and Him crucified and the knowledge of the Godhead in the glorious

103

Trinity" (C. H. Spurgeon). To quote a little further from this prince of preachers:

"The proper study of the Christian is the Godhead. The highest science, the loftiest speculation, the mightiest philosophy, which can engage the attention of a child of God, is the name, the nature, the person, the doings, and the existence of the great God which he calls his Father. There is something exceedingly improving to the mind in a contemplation of the Divinity. It is a subject so vast, that all our thoughts are lost in its immensity; so deep, that our pride is drowned in its infinity. Other subjects we can comprehend and grapple with; in them we feel a kind of self-content, and go on our way with the thought, 'Behold I am wise.' But when we come to this master science, finding that our plumbline cannot sound its depth, and that our eagle eye cannot see its height, we turn away with the thought 'I am but of yesterday and know nothing'" (Sermon on Mal. 3:6).

Yes, the incomprehensibility of the Divine nature should teach us humility, caution and reverence. After all our searchings and meditations we have to say with Job, "Lo, these are parts of His ways: but how little a portion is heard of Him!" (26:14). When Moses besought Jehovah for a sight of His glory, He answered him "I will proclaim the name of the Lord before thee" (Ex. 33:19), and, as another has said, "the name is the collection of His attributes." Rightly did the Puritan John Howe declare, "The notion therefore we can hence form of His glory, is only such as we may have of a large volume by a brief synopsis, or of a spacious country by a little landscape. He hath here given us a true report of Himself, but not a full; such as will secure our apprehensions—being guided thereby—from error, but not from ignorance. We can apply our minds to contemplate the several perfections whereby the blessed God discovers to us His being, and can in our thoughts attribute them all to Him, though we have still but low and defective conceptions of each one. Yet so far as our apprehensions can correspond to the discovery that He affords us of His several excellencies, we have a present view of His glory."

As the difference is indeed great between the knowledge of God which His saints have in this life and that which they shall have in Heaven, yet, as the former should not be undervalued because it is imperfect, so the latter is not to be magnified above its reality. True, the Scripture declares that we shall see "face to face" and "know" even as we are known (I Cor. 13:12), but to infer from this that we shall then know God as fully as He knows us, is to be misled by the mere sound of words, and to disregard that restriction of the same which the subject necessarily requires. There is a vast difference between the saints being glorified and their being made Divine. In their glorified state, Christians will still be finite creatures, and therefore, never able to fully comprehend the infinite God.

"The saints in heaven will see God with the eye of the mind, for He will be always invisible to the bodily eye; and will see Him more clearly than they could see Him by reason and faith, and more extensively than all His works and dispensations had hitherto revealed Him; but their minds will not be so enlarged as to be capable of contemplating at once, or in detail, the whole excellence of His nature. To comprehend infinite perfection, they must become infinite themselves. Even in Heaven, their knowledge will be partial, but at the same time their happiness will be complete, because their knowledge will be perfect in this sense, that it will be adequate to the capacity of the subject, although it will not exhaust the

105

fulness of the object. We believe that it will be progressive, and that as their views expand, their blessedness will increase; but it will never reach a limit beyond which there is nothing to be discovered; and when ages after ages have passed away, He will still be the incomprehensible God" (John Dick, 1840).

Second, from a review of the perfections of God, it appears that He is an all-sufficient Being. He is all-sufficient in Himself and to Himself. As the First of beings, He could receive nothing from another, nor be limited by the power of another. Being infinite, He is possessed of all possible perfection. When the Triune God existed all alone, He was all to Himself. His understanding, His love, His energies, found an adequate object in Himself. Had He stood in need of anything external, He had not been independent, and therefore would not have been God. He created all things, and that "for Himself" (Col. 1:16), yet it was not in order to supply a lack, but that He might communicate life and happiness to angels and men, and admit them to the vision of His glory. True, He demands the allegiance and services of His intelligent creatures, yet He derives no benefit from their offices, all the advantage redounds to themselves: Job 22:2,3. He makes use of means and instruments to accomplish His ends, yet not from a deficiency of power, but often times to more strikingly display His power through the feebleness of the instruments.

The all-sufficiency of God makes Him to be the Supreme Object which is ever to be sought unto. True happiness consists only in the enjoyment of God. His favour is life, and His loving kindness is better than life. "The Lord is my portion, saith my soul; therefore will I hope in Him" (Lam. 3:24); our perceptions of His love, His grace, His glory, are the chief objects of the saints' desire

106

and the springs of their highest satisfaction. "There be many that say, Who will show us any good? Lord, lift Thou up the light of Thy countenance upon us. Thou hast put gladness in my heart, more than in the time that their corn and their wine increased" (Psa. 4:6,7). Yea, the Christian, when in his right mind, is able to say, "Although the fig tree shall not blossom, neither shall fruit be in the vines; the labour of the olive shall fail, and the fields shall yield no meat; the flock shall be cut off from the fold, and there shall be no herd in the stalls: yet I will rejoice in the Lord, I will joy in the God of my salvation" (Hab. 3:17,18).

Third, from a review of the perfections of God, it appears that He is the Supreme Sovereign of the universe. It has been rightly said that, "No dominion is so absolute as that which is founded on creation. He who might not have made any thing, had a right to make all things according to His own pleasure. In the exercise of His uncontrolled power, He has made some parts of the creation mere inanimate matter, of grosser or more refined texture, and distinguished by different qualities, but all inert and unconscious. He has given organization to other parts, and made them susceptible of growth and expansion, but still without life in the proper sense of the term. To others He has given not only organization, but conscious existence, organs of sense and self-motive power. To these He has added in man the gift of reason, and an immortal spirit, by which he is allied to a higher order of beings who are placed in the superior regions. Over the world which He has created, He sways the scepter of omnipotence. 'I praised and honoured Him that liveth forever, whose dominion is an everlasting dominion, and His kingdom is from generation to generation: and all the inhabitants of the earth are reputed as nothing: and

He doeth according to His will in the army of heaven, and among the inhabitants of the earth: and none can stay His hand, or say unto Him, What doeth Thou?' Dan. 4:34,35" (John Dick).

A creature, considered as such, has no rights. He can demand nothing from his Maker; and in whatever manner he may be treated, has no title to complain. Yet, when thinking of the absolute dominion of God over all, we ought never to lose sight of His moral perfections. God is just and good, and ever does that which is right. Nevertheless, He exercises His sovereignty according to His own imperial and righteous pleasure. He assigns each creature his place as seemeth good in His own sight. He orders the varied circumstances of each according to His own counsels. He moulds each vessel according to His own uninfluenced determination. He has mercy on whom He will, and whom He will He hardens. Wherever we are, His eye is upon us. Whoever we are, our life and everything is held at His disposal. To the Christian, He is a tender Father; to the rebellious sinner He will yet be a consuming fire. "Now unto the King eternal, immortal, invisible, the only wise God, be honour and glory for ever and ever. Amen" (I Tim. 1:17).